W
to Budapest

1

Budapest – Spice of Europe.
Find out more by scanning
the QR code

Interior, Matthias Church
© SteveAllenPhoto/iStockphoto.com

Getting to Budapest

Ferenc Liszt International Airport is 22 km southeast of the city centre. **Terminal 2** (only terminal in service) **info** – www.bud.hu/en.

Bus and metro

The cheapest options. Buy tickets from BKK service points in Terminal 2 arrivals hall (post office on the mezzanine level, Relay newsagents, ticket machines at bus stop).

Shuttlebus 100E direct to Deák Ferenc tér in the city centre (1hr journey). Every 30min, between 5am and 0.30am Special fare Ft900 (passes not accepted).

Bus 200E to the metro terminus Kőbánya-Kispest, take line 3 (blue, Újpest Központ direction) via Deák Ferenc tér in the centre (where you can change to metro lines 1 and 2). Between 4am and 11pm: every 8-12min during the day, every 25min evenings. Ft350 including change onto metro), price on bus Ft450.

Night bus 900 to Dél-Pesti Autóbus-zgarázs (bus station), between 11pm and 4am. Every 30–60min. For the city centre, get off at Bajcsy-Zsilinszky út and take bus 950 or 950A via Deák Ferenc tér. Ft530 (including change onto the metro).

Airport minibus/Shuttlebus

The easiest option if this is your first visit to Budapest. The airport's official minibus will drop you off wherever you want in the city and there is no extra charge for luggage. Departures 24hr, every 30min. Pre-ordering 24hrs in advance is recommended: ✆ (1) 550 0000 or www.minibud.hu/en/shuttle. Buy tickets at the miniBUD counters in the arrivals hall. Pay in forints or euros. Price according to the number of passengers: €19.50 for one, €7 per person for three.

Taxi

Főtaxi is the airport's official taxi service. Booths (yellow) at the exits from Terminals 2A, 2B. Allow around Ft7,600 to the centre, or approx. €24. **Info** – ✆ (1) 222 2222 www.fotaxi.hu78.

Metro, bus and tram

Info – www.bkk.hu.
Hours – 4.30am-11.50pm + night service.
Ticket prices – Ft 350 (Ft 450 on the bus, with the right money). Tickets must be validated before travel ♿ p. 117.
Useful passes:
3-day ticket – Valid for the whole Budapest transport network, including night services: Ft 4,150.
Budapest Kártya (Budapest Card) – Valid for the whole Budapest transport network; free or reduced price entry in most of the museums. Ft 6,490 for 24hr, Ft 9,990 48hr and Ft 12,990 72hr. ♿ p. 114.

Tram in front of the Central Market
© mikeinlondon/iStockphoto.com

Unmissable

Our picks for must-see sites

4

Parliament Building★★★
Map C3 – ♿ p. 38

Gellért Baths★★★
Map D7–8 – ♿ p. 31

Chain Bridge★★
Map C5 – ♿ p. 34

Castle District★★★
Map B4–5 – ♿ p. 20

Museum of Fine Arts★★★
Map F/G1–2 – ♿ p. 52

Buda Castle★★★
Map C5 – 👆 p. 14

**Dohány Street
Synagogue★★**
Map E5 – 👆 p. 62

State Opera House★★
Map E4 – 👆 p. 44

5

Széchenyi Baths★★★
Map G1 – ✐ p. 55

New York Café ★
Map F5 – 👆 p. 64

Our top picks

💜 **Admire the panoramic view of the Danube** from the terrace of Buda Castle. Or from the even higher dome of the magnificent Hungarian National Gallery, which occupies a wing of the castle. ♿ *See p. 17.*

💜 **Experience the style of a bygone era in a Hungarian café** with its faded grandeur and air of Old Europe. One of our favourites is Ruszwurm Cukrászda, with decor that hasn't changed since 1827. But that's just a suggestion – everyone will have their own favourite. ♿ *See p. 90.*

💜 **Give your wellbeing a boost with a day at the baths.** Therapeutic thermal baths, relaxation pools, lap pools, hammams, massages... The hardest thing will be to choose which one and what kind of mood: Turkish, Rococo, more contemporary? ♿ *See p. 105.*

💜 **See how far things have changed at the House of Terror Museum**, a harrowing exploration of the dark years of Communism, during the time of mass deportations, deprivations of liberty and other weapons of dictatorship. ♿ *See p. 47.*

💜 **Take an evening stroll along the Danube**, following the Danube Promenade, where tourists and locals come to watch the sun setting over Buda, its bridges and its castle. ♿ *See p. 61.*

💜 **Enjoy a concert at the Franz Liszt Academy of Music** and admire the Art Nouveau decor while allowing yourself to be carried away by the music. The best symphony orchestras in the country perform works here by Liszt, Bartók, Kodály and foreign composers. ♿ *See p. 101.*

💜 **Visit one of the city's covered markets** to browse and perhaps buy fresh produce and/or traditional

© Jon Arnold Images/hemis.fr

Franz Liszt Academy of Music

© Patrice Hauser/hemis.fr

Café Gerbeaud

products. Try the Central Market Hall (the largest and most impressive), the Downtown Market on Hold utca for its slightly 'boho' feel, or the Fény Utca Market, which is still the real Hungarian deal. *See p. 28, 40 and 98.*

💜 **See the remnants of Communism in Memento Park**. The last occupying Soviet soldier left Hungary in 1991. The park is a refuge for gigantic statues and dismantled monuments of the Commnist era. A replica of Stalin's boots presides over the entrance. *See p. 77.*

💜 **Do the rounds of the Secessionist buildings** and discover their amazing interiors. Special mention goes to the Museum of Applied Arts, not forgetting the vast array of Art Nouveau objects and furniture at the House of Hungarian Art Nouveau. *See p. 66 and 39.*

💜 **Bump into a bronze statue on your way around the city.** The city is absolutely crowded with them. *See for example p. 66 and 74.*

💜 **Rub shoulders with young hipsters in a 'ruin bar' in Erzsébetváros,** the old Jewish quarter, where buildings that were abandoned during the Communist era have been converted into late-night bars for party people. The decor is as unusual as the ambience. *See p. 102.*

Budapest in 3 days

DAY 1

▶ **Morning**

Take the Buda funicular at the foot of the Chain Bridge to climb up to **Buda Castle**★★★ *(p. 14)* and discover the view over the city and the Danube. Inside, visit one of the two museums: the **Hungarian National Gallery**★★ *(p. 17)* dedicated to Hungarian art from 1800 to today, or the **Budapest History Museum**★ *(p. 18)*, retracing the history of the city.

▶ **Afternoon**

After a lunch in the old district of **Várnegyed**★★★ *(p. 20)*, just beside the castle, wander through small, pretty restored lanes, not forgetting to stop at **Matthias Church**★★ *(p. 22)*, the city's most visited church for its magnificent interior.

▶ **Evening**

Head back down towards the **Chain Bridge**★★ *(p. 34)* and walk across to

Chain Bridge on a summer evening, Gresham Palace in the background

© titoslack/iStockphoto.com

8

Budapest with children

Preempt any moaning and dragging of feet with these child-friendly options: **Széchenyi Baths**★★★ *(p. 55),* **Budapest Zoo** *(p. 54) and the **ice rink** in City Park (p. 54) ;* **Margaret Island**★★ *(and its various outdoor activities) p. 70, spotting the different façades in* **Váci utca**★ *(p. 59) or taking photos in* **Memento Park**★ *(p. 77), explore the Buda Hills on the* **Children's Railway**★ *(p. 76).*

---

take full advantage of the view over the Danube and Pest, then dine in one of the restaurants on the **Danube Promenade**★★ *(p. 61)*.

DAY 2

▶ **Morning**

Discover the historic centre of Pest, starting with the neighbourhood of **Lipótváros**★★★ *(p. 38)*, where you can visit the **Parliament Building**★★★ *(p. 38)*, one of the icons of the city.

When you come out, wander through this pleasant neighbourhood with its leafy squares, its antique shops on **Falk Miksa utca** (ⓒ *p. 94*), and, for Art Nouveau enthusiasts, the **House of Hungarian Art Nouveau**★ *(p. 39)*.

▶*Afternoon*

Have lunch in one of the many restaurants in the **Belváros**★★ neighbourhood *(p. 86)*, the other beating heart of the town's historic centre. Make the most of the shopping options, especially around the pedestrian street **Váci utca**★ *(p. 59)*, but don't linger too long if you want to visit the **Dohány Street Synagogue**★★ *(p. 62)* as it closes at 6pm in summer.

▶*Evening*

At the end of the afternoon, head for the old Jewish quarter, **Erzsébetváros**★ *(p. 62)*, and take a stroll through the streets – it's a popular haunt for partygoers. Dine in one of the district's hip restaurants before ending your evening in a *romkocsma* ('ruin bar', *p. 102*).

DAY 3

▶*Morning*

Walk up **Andrássy út** ★★ *(p. 44)*, one of Budapest's grand boulevards. Depending on your interests, you can visit the **State Opera House**★★, the **Hungarian House of Photography**★, the **Franz Liszt Museum**★ or the **House of Terror**★★, which are all in the same area. Have lunch in **Liszt Ferenc tér** *(p. 47)*, a large tree-filled square lined with cafés and restaurants.

▶*Afternoon*

Take the metro to **Heroes' Square** and visit the **Museum of Fine Arts**★★★ *(p. 52),* which houses remarkable collections of paintings by the European masters, including many from Hungary in the 'Old Hungarian Collection'. Next, head to **Széchenyi Baths**★★★ *(p. 55)*, one of the largest bath complexes, in a setting that simply could not be more baroque.

▶*Evening*

Dine in the area around **St Stephen's Basilica**★★ *(p. 42)*, especially lively in the evenings with its many bars and restaurants. The location will suit lovers of live performance, who can easily get back to the entertainment district from here. **Andrássy út** *(p. 101) is* a stone's throw away. Now's the time to treat yourself to a concert. Now's the time to treat yourself to a concert or show.

9

Day 4: around the city

Discover some of the more intimate museums and unusual sites, such as **Memento Park**★ *with its monumental statues from the Communist era (p. 77),* **Kerepesi Cemetery**★ *(and its dramatic tombs, p. 65), the* **Ludwig Museum of Contemporary Art** ★★ *(and its involvement with the Hungarian avant-garde, p. 68)... To stretch your legs a little outside there's always* **Margaret Island**★★ *(and its many attractions, p. 70) or head for the* **Buda Hills** *(with their hiking trails and 500m 'peaks', p. 76), particularly tempting in summer when the heat in the city streets can be heavy and stifling.*

Discovering Budapest

Fisherman's Bastion
© tunart/iStockphoto.com

Budapest today

Your first impressions of Budapest might leave you wondering whether this really is 'the pearl of the Danube' whose charm and beauty people rave about? Isn't it a little noisy, aren't there too many cars and crumbling façades? And then you look again and things become a little clearer. The Hungarian capital is certainly a city of contrasts, but this is absolutely part of its charm. Sumptuous buildings from the time of the Austro-Hungarian Compromise and Secessionist architectural splendours rub shoulders with buildings pock–marked by bullets. Brand new shopping centres and contemporary structures designed by architects of international renown stand beside empty plots awaiting new, cutting-edge buildings.

Buda and Pest

Budapest is a beautiful and fascinating city, and one that is separated into two quite distinct entities by the majestic **River Danube**, Buda on the western bank and Pest on the eastern. One of the most evocative and romantic of European rivers, the Danube flows south, so a little confusingly Buda is also said to be on the right bank and Pest on the left. The green hills of **Buda** support the imposing **Castle**. The jaw-dropping vista from the top explains why Budapest and the banks of the the Danube are listed as a UNESCO World Heritage site. The **Buda Castle District**, including the magnificent

Matthias Church with its glazed tiles, also draws the tourists. Although very charming, with its small cobbled lanes and immaculately restored monuments, it is one of the only areas in the city to feel almost slightly artificial. On the other side of the Danube, **Pest** is unquestionably *the* Austro-Hungarian city par excellence.

A city under restoration

Pest has escaped the 'city-museum' aspect of other European metropolis. **Erzsébetváros**, for example, which contains some very beautiful synagogues, hasn't undergone the kind of tourism-driven reconstruction as a 'Jewish Quarter' as has been the case in Prague. It is still a genuine centre of activity where brand new buildings owned by foreign investors mingle with old and rather faded ones, some of them vacant and run down and converted into the 'ruin bars' which have been fashionable since the early 2000s. The city centre, which lay dormant for a time while recovering from the torments of the Second World War and Russian domination, now has a real sense of energy. But this energy seems to be spreading out more slowly than in other Eastern European capitals. There has been no rehabilitation of the city as a whole, but instead a plethora of often private initiatives has been cropping up all over the place. The beginning of the prestigious avenue **Andrássy út**, where the opera house and theatre

12

district are located, has undergone a complete facelift. This also applies to some parts of **Belváros**, such as Váci utca and Deák Ferenc utca, where big luxury brands jostle for prime spots among gleaming façades. Not far away, the worlds of politics, administration and business are concentrated in the grand district of **Lipótváros**, where you bump into a monument, statue or museum at every turn. The imposing neo-Gothic **Parliament Building** is one of those structures that were built to compete with Vienna, Budapest's eternal rival. Elsewhere, the building restorations are more random. But it's worth making a point to look up at the façades – you might be surprised by the great architectural diversity that is the norm in Pest.

The pleasures of Budapest

Spending a few hours in the baths is one of Budapest's must-dos. Feeling a little tired and need to relax? Do as the Hungarians do and go to the baths. Beneath the city are many underground thermal springs, which have been in use since Roman times, with bathing raised to a fine art especially during the Ottoman occupation. You move from bath to bath, from hot to cold, through interiors that range in style from ostentatious neo-baroque to the purest Ottoman. And when you finally tear yourself away, why not treat yourself to one of the famous Hungarian **pastries**? It's a perfect opportunity to soak up the 'Old Europe' atmosphere of one of the capital's **cafés**. Duly revived, you will

© Subodh Agnihotri/iStockphoto.com

13

Váci utca decorated for Christmas, Belváros

be ready to plan your evening. The glorious State Opera House is one 'must' for lovers of classical music. But the problem is choosing between all the other options – music is very important to the Hungarian soul. As a result Budapest is simply brimming with venues offering classical, jazz, folk ... while the contemporary music scene is also well catered for. The annual **Sziget Festival** on Óbuda Island provides ample proof of this. So, Budapest is all these things: an extraordinary city architecturally, with monuments and statues in abundance and all the charm of a bygone era, but also forward looking, with a distinct energy and buzz. Now it's your turn to experience it.

Buda Castle★★★
(Budai Vár)

Built in the 13C, significantly remodelled under the Habsburgs and rebuilt after the Second World War, this imposing castle dominates the hill that rises around fifty metres above the Danube. It houses, among other things, the Hungarian National Gallery, which is dedicated to the best of Hungarian art.

▶**Access:** bus 16, 16A, 105 Clark Ádám tér or 🚋 19, 41 Clark Ádám tér, then climb the steps up to the castle or take the funicular or Budapest Castle Bus which has 5 stops around the castle district (9am–4pm – Ft2,100, free with the Budapest Card). *Area map p. 16. Detachable map C5.*
🖰 *Addresses p. 82 and 94.*

FUNICULAR

(Sikló)

7.30am–10pm – daily Ft1,200, round trip Ft1,800.
Connecting Clark Ádám tér and the castle, the funicular has been a godsend to tired feet since 1870. Destroyed during the Second World War, an identical replica was made in 1983, with red and yellow wooden cars. The queue can be quite long.

SZENT GYÖRGY TÉR

(Szent György Square)

This square lies in front of the main entrance to the castle. On the right you can see the neoclassical **Sándor Palace (Sándor palota)**. Formerly the Hungarian prime minister's residence, it now houses the office and official residence of the president of the republic. The **changing of the guard** takes place in front of the palace, on the hour between 9am and 5pm.

Next door, the **Court Theatre of Buda (Várszínház)** with its classical façade, used to be a Carmelite church and convent but was dissolved and converted in 1782. The National Dance Theatre, which was based here for a time, is now performing in various other venues in the city while waiting to move into the Millenáris Teátrum (🖰 *p. 29*). The Court Theatre building, which has been undergoing renovation for years, will ultimately become the office of the prime minister. Opposite the building, you can see ruins dating from the Middle Ages.

CASTLE EXTERIOR

A bird of prey with its wings spread out and a sword in its talons seems about to take flight from a pillar of the neo-baroque gate to the castle grounds. This is the mythical **turul**

(pronounced *toorool*) emblem of the Hungarian Magyar tribes. The baroque façade of the Royal Palace is over 300m long and overlooks the Danube. A central dome sits between two impressive wings. Presiding over the vast panoramic terrace is the **Equestrian Statue of Prince Eugene of Savoy (Savoyai Jenő szobor)**, one of the liberators of Hungary from the Ottoman Turks. Two scenes from the Battle of Zenta are represented on the pedestal (1697). Continue along the

terrace until you are looking down on the river: the **view★★** is magnificent with, from left to right, Margaret Island, the Parliament Building, the Chain Bridge, St Stephen's Basilica, Elisabeth Bridge, Liberty Bridge, and then, in the distance, Gellért Hill, the Citadel and the Liberty Statue.
At the bottom of Castle Hill, the gardens **(várkert)** are open to the public once more. Inaugurated at the end of the 19C, ravaged by bombardments in the Second World

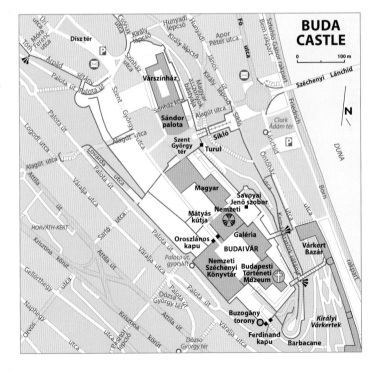

16

Building Buda Castle

King Béla IV, who ruled Hungary 1235-1270, built a fortress here to protect Buda from a Mongol invasion. It was extended during the reign of Sigismund of Luxembourg (1387-1437), Holy Roman Emperor, but it enjoyed its golden age during the reign of Matthias Corvinus (1458-1490). This brilliant and cultured king promoted art and science and rebuilt much of the castle in the Renaissance style. However, in 1686 it was all but destroyed in the struggle against the occupying Turks during the Siege of Buda. In the 18C and 19C successive Habsburg rulers set about elevating the castle to the status of royal residence. First Maria Theresa of Austria made improvements in the baroque style, then King Franz Joseph entrusted the job of further remodelling in a neo-baroque style to Hungarian architects Miklós Ybl and Alajos Hauszmann, although in fact the king visited only rarely.

War and turned into a 'Youth Park' during the Communist era, they have now been restored to their former glory and contain several different spaces and buildings, including the **Castle Garden Bazaar★ (Várkert Bazár)**, built by architect Miklós Ybl in a neo-Renaissance style and now renovated and hosting temporary exhibitions *(www.varkertbazar.hu – daily except Mon 10am–5.30pm. Info at the glass kiosk in front of the National Gallery. Access also possible from the quay: Ybl Miklós tér 2–6 – 🚋 19). Take the passage to the right of the entrance to the National Gallery.* The main attraction of the forecourt is the **Matthias Fountain★ (Mátyás-kút)**, which is impossible to miss. This sculptural group in bronze, the work of Alajos Stróbl (1904), represents the king, who is shown standing resplendent in front of a stag in a hunting scene and was inspired by a ballad by 19C Romantic poet and dramatist Mihály Vörösmarty. In it Matthias meets a beautiful young girl named Ilonka while out hunting. On the left after the fountain, you

reach the internal courtyard through the **Lions' Gate (Oroszlános kapu)**, whose entrance is guarded by two stone lions. Standing in the centre of this beautiful courtyard you will be surrounded by some majestic buildings, in particular the **National Széchenyi Library (Nemzeti Széchenyi Könyvtár)**. At the end of the courtyard, walk through the entrance of the **Budapest History Museum (♿ p. 18)** and down the stairs leading to the southern ramparts and the **Mace Tower (Buzogány-torony)**, a remnant of the medieval fortifications. You can leave the castle grounds through a gate beside the tower, the **Ferdinand Gate (Ferdinand kapu)**, and see the **Déli Rondella**, a 14C and 15C defensive structure.

HUNGARIAN NATIONAL GALLERY★★

(Magyar Nemzeti Galéria)
Szent György tér – ℘ (1) 201 9082 – mng.hu – Tue-Sun 10am-6pm (including access to the dome) – closed Mon – Ft1,800 (free access

to the permanent exhibition with the Budapest Card) – audioguide in English Ft800; temporary exhibitions Ft3,200.

Ⓐ The collection covering the period from the Middle Ages to the end of the 17C has been transferred to the Museum of Fine Arts (Ⓖ p. 52). In 2021 the Hungarian National Gallery will move to Városliget (City Park), to a new building designed by Japanese architectural firm Sanaa (ligetbudapest.hu/institution/new-national-gallery).

This museum is dedicated to Hungarian art from the 19C to today. Notable among the 19C painters are **Mihály Munkácsy** (1844–1900) and **László Paál** (1846–1879) who were firm friends. Both were influenced by French painters and Munkácsy studied in Berlin, Munich and Paris. His *Last Day of a Condemned Man* subscribes to a realist, dramatic aesthetic; in contrast, his *Woman Carrying Brushwood*, painted during a stay in Barbizon in northern France is more lyrical. Paál was very influenced by the Barbizon school, which is particularly evident in his landscape paintings *(Noon, Path in the Forest of Fontainebleau, Landscape with Cows).* Look out also for **Pál Színyei Merse**'s *Picnic in May,* a favourite subject among the Impressionists. The museum also brings together monumental works on historical subjects, such as **Gyula Benczúr** *The Baptism of Vajk* (the future King Stephen I of Hungary). The museum hosts temporary exhibitions as well.

Ⓐ When the weather is clear, make sure you climb up to the **dome**. It has been restored and there is an amazing 360° **view★★** from the terrace out over Budapest *(May–Oct 10am–5pm, access from the 3rd and 4th floors of the gallery).*

BUDAPEST HISTORY MUSEUM★

(Budapesti Történeti Múzeum)
Szent György tér 2 – ℘ (1) 487 8800 – www.btm.hu – Mar–Oct 10am–6pm, Nov–Feb 10am–4pm – closed Mon – Ft2,000 (free with the Budapest Card) – audioguide in English Ft1,200.
'Budapest through the ages' sums up the content of this museum. Prehistory, antiquity, the Middle Ages, the modern era and the construction of the castle are all covered in a series of rooms displaying various collections: archaeological finds, jewellery, ceramics, objects from everyday life, and so on. Worth seeing in particular is the **Gothic sculpture room** *(ground floor)*, which contains some very beautiful limestone statues, often very expressive and well-presented with special lighting (pick up a map at the entrance to the room to follow the numbering of the pieces). The lower and underground sections of the castle date back to the medieval era and house rooms with beautiful ribbed vaulting (an impressive hall with a tiled stove). Most date from the time of Sigismund of Luxembourg, who ruled from 1387 to 1437. Also notable is the **Palace Chapel**, built in the 14C under the reign of the Anjou kings. In the centre is a three-part retable illuminated by three picture windows.

Hungarian National Gallery

18

Várnegyed★★★
(Buda Castle District)

After a stroll around the castle ground, you might want to take in a gallery or museum or just enjoy the views. It's also worth wandering around the old Castle District to see the buildings and monuments and to do a little shopping. There are plenty of places to eat if you're feeling peckish – you just need to choose between the street food vendors and the more well-established eateries.

▶**Access:** bus 16, 16A, 116 Dísz tér; 🚋 19, 41 Clark Ádám tér, then climb the steps up or take the funicular (♿ *p. 14)*; Ⓜ 2 Széll Kálmán tér.
Area map opposite. Detachable map B4–5.
♿ *Addresses p. 82, 90, 94 and 108.*

TÁRNOK UTCA

(Treasurer's Street)
A busy trading area in the Middle Ages, Treasurer's Street (a reference to the king's chief financial advisor), is lined with beautiful buildings with painted façades, decorative corbels and baroque ornamentation. Cafés, shops selling souvenirs and traditional Hungarian embroideries…. There's no doubt this street is well established on the tourist trail. Some of the building façades are worthy of attention, such as the very colourful **no. 14** (Café Tárnok), which dates from the 14C and 15C and was restored in the 1950s.

PHARMACY MUSEUM

(Arany Sas Patikamúzeum)
Tárnok utca 18 – ℘ (1) 375 9772 – semmelweis.museum.hu – Mar–Oct, weekends & public holidays 10am–5.30pm; Nov–Feb 10am–3.30pm – closed Mon – Ft800 – guided tour Ft1,000 (ask for info).

A 15C merchant's house became the Arany Sas Pharmacy ('Golden Eagle' Pharmacy, as you can see from the wrought-iron sign above the door) in the mid 18C. Today this small museum displays pharmaceutical objects, pots and instruments from the 16C to the 19C. Two of the rooms are particularly interesting: the recreation of an 18C apothecary and a laboratory that looks more like an alchemist's lair. A little further along Tárnok utca, look to your left down **Balta köz** (Axe Passage), a small side street and supposedly named for some violent 'goings-on', a street fight with axes in the 15C involving one or more of the powerful Hunyadi family.

SZENTHÁROMSÁG TÉR

(Trinity Square)
The main square of the Castle District owes its name to **Holy Trinity Statue**★ **(Szentháromság szobor)**, which stands in the centre. This monument (14m tall and made of limestone) was

20

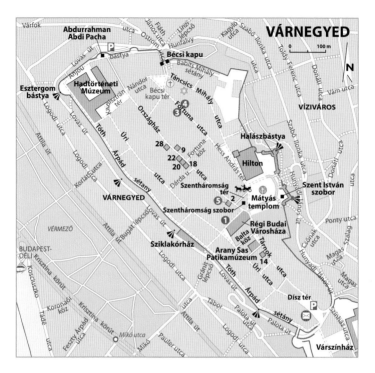

WHERE TO EAT
Alabárdos................. ⑤   21......................... ④
Café Pierrot................. ③

WHERE TO DRINK
Ruszwurm Cukrászda........ ①

erected in the 18C to commemorate the plague epidemics of the 17C and 18C. It was the tradition at the time for survivors to erect a monument in gratitude to God for being spared. On the right side of the square is Matthias Church while at the corner of Szentháromság utca is a baroque palace built at the end of the 17C by an Italian architect, which used to house the **Old Buda Town Hall (Régi Budai Városháza)**, but is now

Gothic niches

In several streets of the Castle District, you can see seats cut into Gothic niches or recesses set into the walls of porches and often in groups of three. At first sight, they look like the stalls in a medieval church, such as were used by the canons. So to see them in a residential house seems somewhat curious, for example in the street Úri utca (⚫ p.28), at nos. 31, 32, 34 and 42. Several suggestions have been put forward to explain their purpose, including that they were used to display goods, as places for servants to wait patiently for their masters or that they were simply a bit of a fashion, with each house owner trying to impress his neighbour.

an educational institute. A clock tower rises up from what used to be a chapel. On the corner, in a niche beneath the oriel window, is a statue of Athena, protector of the city. She holds a sculpted shield in her right hand showing the Buda coat of arms.

MATTHIAS CHURCH★★

(Mátyás templom)
Szentháromság tér - ℘ (1) 488 7716 - www.matyas-templom.hu - 9am-5pm, Sat 9am-2.30pm, Sun 1pm-5pm - Ft1,500; guided tours can be requested and reserved min. 3 days in advance, see website - Ft2,500 (up to 5 people).

Originally called the Church of Our Lady of the Assumption, it received its current name in 19C in homage to **King Matthias Corvinus**, who added his own extensions to the building and also celebrated his weddings here: firstly in 1461 to Catherine of Poděbrady, princess of Bohemia; then a second time in 1476 to Beatrice, daughter of Ferdinand I of Aragon, king of Naples.

In the 13C King Béla IV built a three-nave basilica on the site of a church dedicated to the Virgin. Some years later, in 1309, Charles Robert of Anjou was crowned king here (after his coronation by the bishop of Esztergom in Székesfehérvár, as tradition dictated). The building acquired its current dimensions during the reigns of Sigismund of Luxembourg (14C) and Matthias (15C), who is responsible for adding the south tower.

The Turks, who ruled Buda in 1541, destroyed the Christian interiors and turned the church into a mosque, covering its walls with carpets. Freed from the Turks by the Christian armies in 1686, King Leopold I gave the Church of Our Lady to the Jesuits, who added some baroque elements. In 1867, Franz Joseph I, the Austrian emperor, and his wife Elisabeth ('Sisi') were crowned rulers of Hungary here. Franz Liszt composed the *Coronation Mass* for this event, and conducted it himself. Franz Joseph commissioned architect Frigyes Schulek to restore the church's Gothic elements, work that took some twenty years to complete. After the Second World War, a further twenty years of restoration work took place. Today

Matthias Church

the church has regained its former glory and is one of the most popular places to visit in the capital.

Exterior

On the main façade, **Matthias Tower** soars 80m up into the sky. Quadrangular at the base, it becomes octagonal at higher levels and ends in a slender spire. To the left of the main portal, the smaller **Béla Tower** is in the Romanesque style.

Above the portal is a tympanum representing a Madonna and Child between two angels. The roofs of the church are covered with beautiful multicoloured glazed tiles. This type of roofing was common in the 15C. The south portal, or **Mary Gate** (on the right), dates back to the time of Louis I of Hungary. A bas-relief on the pediment, the *Dormition of the Virgin*, represents the Virgin kneeling between the apostles. At the top of the vault, God reigns over the world with the royal crown and terrestrial globe. On either side of the portal is a statue of St Stephen and Saint Ladislaus (King Ladislaus I).

Interior

Enter through the Mary Gate. Once inside, you will be greeted by a profusion of paintings. The vaults, walls and pillars are beautifully decorated with geometric and plant motifs in a neo-medieval style. In the nave, flags from the different provinces of Hungary refer back to the 1867 coronation. The neo-Gothic high altar of the choir shows a statue of the Virgin in a mandorla illuminated by golden rays. The Four Evangelists

and Church Fathers are represented on the pulpit.
Make a circuit of the church, starting from the left of the choir:
St Ladislaus Chapel – Frescoes of the life of the saint, an 11C knight-king, painted by Károly Lotz.
Holy Trinity Chapel – It contains the sarcophagi of the Árpád king Béla III and his wife, Agnes of Antioch.
Saint Emeric (Imre) Chapel – Three-winged altarpiece. On the central panel, the prince-saint Emeric (killed by a boar while hunting) is surrounded by his father, Saint Stephen (King Stephen I), and his Venetian tutor, the Benedictine bishop Saint Gerard.
Baptismal fonts – This beautiful work in sculpted stone consists of a basin supported by four small columns with a lion at their base and is covered with a bronze lid.
Loreto Chapel – Enclosed by a beautiful wrought-iron gate, this chapel is dedicated to the cult of the Madonna. Notice the red marble statue of the Madonna and Child wearing the imperial crown of Austria.
Ecclesiastical Art Museum (Egyháztörténeti Gyűjtemény) – *Via steps in the chapel to the right of the choir.* Cross the crypt (red marble sarcophagus containing the bones of the kings of the Árpád dynasty found in Székesfehérvár, coats of arms of the Knights of the Order of Malta) before reaching St Stephen's Chapel (bust of Elisabeth of Austria, nicknamed 'Sisi', in Carrara marble at the entrance) which displays the reliquary bust of the saint. The stained-glass windows depict the

saints and the blessed of Hungary. A spiral staircase leads up to the Royal Oratory with displays featuring the coronation regalia. Next is a gallery displaying sacerdotal vestments and sacred objects (chalices, patens, monstrances…).

STATUE OF SAINT STEPHEN

(Szent István szobor)
This work in bronze by the sculptor Alajos Stróbl (1856–1926) stands in front of the Fisherman's Bastion. The first king of Hungary, Stephen I, is represented on his caparisoned horse, wearing his coronation cape and holding in his right hand the patriarchal cross which symbolises the country's conversion to Christianity. The halo around his head is an allusion to his canonisation in 1083. The imposing neo-Romanesque pedestal is a fine example of sculpted limestone. The bas-reliefs depict significant events from his reign.

FISHERMAN'S BASTION★

(Halászbástya)
Behind Matthias Church – www. fishermansbastion.com – access to the upper floor mid-Mar to end Apr 9am–7pm, beg May to mid-Oct 9am–8pm – Ft1,000 (reduced price with the Budapest Card); mid-Oct to mid-Mar 24hr, no charge.
Built between 1895 and 1902, the Fisherman's Bastion is a collection of neo-Romanesque balconies and and turrets which bring to mind a fairytale castle. Although only just over one hundred years old, the origin of the name is uncertain: it either comes from a fish market that operated nearby in the Middle Ages, or the fishermen's guilds who actively participated in the defence of the city from the original ramparts. The bastion was built to celebrate the city's millenium in 1896; it has never been used for defence. The seven turrets symbolise the seven Magyar tribes, each chief being represented by a statue. During the bastion's construction, the medieval St Michael Chapel was revealed underground and partly incorporated into it. The walk around the terrace is not to be missed and tourists flock here for the extensive **views★★** over the Danube to Pest on the opposite side of the river. There's also a café with tables on the terrace from where you can enjoy the spectacular panorama to the full. And there's a view of the coloured roofs of Matthias Church from here too. At the end of the terrace steps head down to the Víziváros district (👣 *p. 34*).

HILTON HOTEL

The modern architecture of the Budapest branch of this well-known hotel chain (opened in 1977, at the time the first Hilton in a Communist European country) looks rather incongruous in this otherwise heritage-listed environment. It was built on the site of the 13C Dominican St Nicholas monastery and incorporates parts of the old building. In one part of the old church wall you can see a bas-relief paying homage to **Matthias Corvinus** (a copy, the

25

original is in Ortenburg Castle in Germany). The king is shown on his throne with sceptre in hand. Two angels hold the royal crown above his head. You have to enter the hotel to see the remains of the old monastery and cloister.

TÁNCSICS MIHÁLY UTCA★★

(Mihály Táncsics Street)
This street is lined with beautiful baroque and neoclassical houses with coloured façades. It was named after the writer, politician and freedom fighter **Mihály Táncsics** (1799–1884), a hero of the struggle for national independence and supporter of the emancipation of the poor.

VIENNA GATE★

(Bécsi kapu)
The second great gate to the city in former times, the Vienna Gate was rebuilt in 1936 as part of the celebrations for the 250th anniversary of the liberation of Buda. It was known as the Saturday Gate in the Middle Ages, after the market held in front of it every weekend. A plaque inside the gate honours the soldiers of different nationalities who gave their lives in the battles to liberate the city from the Ottoman occupation. The **Monument to the Recapture of Buda** (1936), which shows an angel in the form of a woman brandishing a patriarchal cross, symbolises the victory of the Christian armies assembled by Pope Innocent XI.

FORTUNA UTCA★★

(Fortuna Street)
Another typical street of the Castle District, with historic old buildings and decorative façades.

ORSZÁGHÁZ UTCA

(Országház Street)
The city's main thoroughfare during the Middle Ages, 'Parliament Street' has been so-named since 1790, when the Hungarian parliament sat in a former Clarissine convent at no. 28, today one of the buildings of the National Academy of Sciences. Look for Gothic elements on several of the houses (nos. 2, 9, 18, 20 and 22).

MUSEUM OF MILITARY HISTORY★

(Hadtörténeti Múzeum)
Tóth Árpád Sétány 40 – ☏ (1) 325 1600 – militaria.hu – Apr–Sept 10am–6pm, Oct–Mar 10am–4pm – closed Mon – Ft1,500.
A former barracks built in 1830 is the setting for this museum, heralded by a row of cannons. You'll see all the weapons, uniforms, medals and so on, that you'd expect to find in a military museum, but you can also learn about the role of Hungary in peacekeeping missions – perhaps less well known – during the Vietnam war in particular. The Hungarian Revolution of 1848 that grew into a War of Independence from Austria is covered on the first floor, along with the Second World War and the 1956 Hungarian Revolution – in short, all the major events in which the national army has been involved.

Úri Utca

ÚRI UTCA★★

(Úri Street)

Take a walk along the longest street in the Castle District with a distinctly tranquil, residential feel and see the rows of beautiful houses with baroque façades.

TÓTH ÁRPÁD PROMENADE★

(Tóth Árpád sétány)

Extending from the Esztergom Bastion to **Dísz tér** along the medieval ramparts, the main attraction of the Tóth Árpád Promenade is the **view** it offers over the western neighbourhoods of Buda, from the Buda Hills to Gellért Hill. The national flag flies over **Esztergom Bastion (Esztergom bástya)**, symbolising the end of the Turkish occupation. From here, the **view** in the foreground is of part of Buda, with János Hill to the rear. Walk a little further along the Anjou Bastion and after another row of cannons, you will see a tombstone topped with a turban that belongs to **Abdurrahman Abdi Pasha**, the last governor of Buda. He died defending the city against the Habsburg soldiers. The monument was erected as a form of reconciliation by the family of a Hungarian soldier, György Szabó, who died on the same spot. The inscription reads: 'He was a heroic enemy, may he rest in peace.'

HOSPITAL IN THE ROCK

(Sziklakórház)

Lovas út 4/C – ℘ 707 01 01 01 – www.sziklakorhaz.eu – guided tour only, every hour on the hour 10am–7pm – Ft4,000 (reduced price with the Budapest Card).

During the Second World War and later during the 1956 Revolution, the many underground caves beneath Castle Hill concealed a remarkable underground hospital. Four km in length, it could care for up to 200 patients. You can see the kitchens, the operating theatre, the dormitories and the infirmary, as well as a nuclear bunker. After a short stint as a prison it was 'upgraded' for the nuclear age 1958–1962, but fortunately never had to be used.

SZÉLL KÁLMÁN TÉR

(Széll Kálmán Square)

Detachable map A3 *–* Ⓜ *2 and* 🚋 *4, 6, 19, 56, 56A, 59, 61 Széll Kálmán tér.*

Named **Moszkva tér** (Moscow Square) until 2012, it is an interchange for several underground and overland public transport systems. The square became synonymous with resourcefulness, survival and commerce for a whole generation of Budapesters. It underwent a complete renovation in 2016 with only the roof of the metro station left to still fly the flag for the 1970s. Today the look is contemporary and functional with a fountain in the centre, embodying the tone of the Hungarian capital's new urban future.

◗ *Walk down Dékán utca to find Fény utca.*

Fény Utca Market *(Mon–Fri 6am–6pm, Sat 6am–2pm)* is a popular local market. It is worth consideration as a more interesting place in which to stock up on supplies than the enormous and touristy Vásárcsarnok (Central Market Hall – 👍 *p. 66*). Beneath a large glass roof, there are four floors of vendors offering fruit and vegetables picked that same morning (some organic) and some Hungarian specialities. In May you can find delicious large fleshy strawberries that are rarely seen elsewhere. Head up up to the mezzanine level for charcuterie, sausages, salamis, foie gras, spices... It's a good opportunity to try something new or take a break at one of the small restaurants nearby. Further north on Lövőház street, travel forward in time in the vast **Mammut Shopping Centre** *(Mon–Sat 10am–9pm, Sun 6pm)*. It hosts many different stores (a few of which you'll

recognise) selling all kinds of goods and brands, and a cinema. The top floor is packed with restaurants.

MILLENÁRIS

Detachable map A2–3 *– Fény utca 20–22 –* Ⓜ *2 and* 🚋 *4, 6, 19, 56, 56A, 59, 61 Széll Kálmán tér.*
Next to the shopping centre, the old buildings of this former industrial wasteland have been converted into a cultural complex, with venues for exhibitions, concerts and theatre in the centre of a landscaped park.
The **National Dance Theatre** *(Nemzeti Tancszinhaz – www.tancszinhaz. hu, European modern dance).* For a time this occupied the Court Theatre of Buda (👍 *p. 14*), but has recently moved to the new Millenáris Teátrum.

29

© Juergen Hasenkopf/imageBROKER/age fotostock

Millenáris

Gellérthegy★★

(Gellért Hill)

Situated between Elisabeth Bridge and Liberty Bridge, leafy Gellért Hill (235m) is one of the iconic locations on the western bank of the river. In the 19C its slopes were covered with vineyards which were wiped out by phylloxera, but today it is covered in trees. According to legend, it was a popular place for witches and wizards to meet on the night of the sabbath, but it is named after Saint Gerard who was thrown to his death from here. At the foot of the hill, several thermal springs supply the Gellért and Rudas Baths.

▶**Access:** Ⓜ 4 Szent Gellért tér; 🚊 19, 41, 47, 48, 56, 56A Szent Gellért tér; to get to the hill on foot from Pest, take Liberty Bridge.
Detachable map CD 6–7.
♿ *Addresses p. 82, 90 and 100.*

30

LIBERTY BRIDGE★★

(Szabadság Híd)

D7 Along with the Chain Bridge, this is one of the most interesting bridges in the city. In 1945 it was destroyed by retreating German troops but was restored the year after. With a span of 331m it is the shortest bridge in Budapest and a fine example of iron architecture. Originally called the 'Franz Joseph Bridge', it was opened in 1896 by the emperor himself but renamed symbolically the year it was rebuilt. The four turrets on top of the pillar columns are each decorated with a mythical *turul* bird, while the arches at either end bear the coat of arms of Hungary topped with the Holy Crown.

St Stephen's Day

Every year on 20 August, Hungarians pay homage to their first king, Stephen, also known as King St Stephen. The day is a national holiday celebrating the founding of Hungary. The festivities start with the raising of the Hungarian flag and continue with various concerts and processions, and mass is celebrated. Traditionally in the capital, the Holy Dexter of St Stephen (his right hand) is carried in procession (♿ p. 43) and fireworks are launched at around 9pm from Mount Gellért and several other points, including near the Parliament Building. The crowds begin to gather on the banks of the Danube, particularly on the Pest side, and on the bridges from around 6pm and wait patiently to see the sky over Budapest erupt in a fabulous show that lasts around half an hour. The brilliant colours are reflected in the waters of the river.

GELLÉRT BATHS★★★

(Gellértfürdő)

D7–8 – *Kelenhegyi út 4–6 – ♿ p. 105.*
Part of the same building as the
Gellért Hotel, but independent from
it, this is a large complex of pools
and thermal baths. The **Secessionist**
architecture alone makes them worth
a look. Inside the main baths complex,
the swimming pool replaced the
hotel's winter conservatory in 1934.
Beneath the glass and metal arched
roof, which opens up in summer,
the rectangular pool is framed by
columns decorated with twisting
floral motifs. These columns support a
mezzanine walkway, itself decorated
with green plants and pillars tiled with
Zsolnay porcelain. At the end of the
pool are two small doors which lead,
respectively, to the men's thermal
baths *(férfiak)* and to the women's
baths *(nők),* although they are now
mixed. Look out for the blue mosaics,
medallions, cherubs and fountains in
the pure **Art Deco style**.
The tea rooms (Eszpresszó) in the
adjacent Gellért Hotel offer excellent
pastries. The decor may be slightly
ageing but it doesn't spoil the
pleasure of nibbling a cake here,
cosily cocooned in a charming old-
fashioned armchair in winter, listening
to the pianist, or under one of the sun
umbrellas on the terrace in summer.

CAVE CHURCH

(Sziklatemplom)

D7 – *Szent Gellért rakpart 1 –
📞 (20) 775 2472 – daily except Sun
9.30am–7.30pm – Ft600 audioguide.*
Built in 1926 in the style of the
Sanctuary of Our Lady of Lourdes,
this church accommodated the
Hungarian Christian community of the
Order of Saint Paul until 1951, when
the monks were imprisoned by the
Communists and the cave was closed.
Reopened in 1991 and given back to
the Pauline monks, mass has been
celebrated here every day since then.

LIBERTY STATUE

(Szabadság–szobor)

C7 On a tall limestone pedestal, the
statue of a woman (14m) proudly
holds a palm leaf above her head at
arm's length, seeming to offer it to
the sky. This colossal monument, of a
type found in many Central European
countries, was erected in 1947 in
memory of the liberation of the city
by the soldiers of the Russian Red
Army. There is a fine **view★★** over the
river from the terrace beneath the
statue of both Buda and Pest. To the
right you have a bird's eye view of
Gellért Baths and the hotel.

CITADELLA

(Citadel)

CD7 – *www.citadella.hu - Closed for
works for an indefinite period.*
To the rear of Liberty Statue, this
U–shaped fortress is strategically
positioned on the summit of Gellért
Hill. It was built in 1851 on the orders
of Emperor Franz Joseph I following
the Hungarian revolt of 1848–1849
against the Austrians. The citadel was
used for anti-aircraft defence during
the Second World War. Its doors

were later thrown open to tourists, with a hotel, café and restaurant, a photographic exhibition (covering the period 1850–1945) and a small museum, the **1944 Wax Museum (Panoptikum 1944)**, which occupies the former air raid shelter. Its wax figures arranged in scenes from the Second World War provide an idea of what the citadel was like during the conflict.

You can still climb up to the Citadel and the **view★★★** from the terraces certainly should not be missed. You will find yourself looking down on Buda below and Pest across the river, especially pretty when lit up at night. To the left, in the distance, Margaret Island, one of the green spaces of the city, is clearly visible.

JUBILEE PARK

(Jubileumi Park)

C7 This park was opened for the fortieth anniversary of the October Revolution. It is laid out in a natural style, with trees and grass and paths that wend there way between flowerbeds and the modern stone and metal artworks and sculptures that are dotted about.

SZENT GELLÉRT MONUMENT

(Szent Gellért Emlékmű)

C6 Gellért (Saint Gerard in English) was the first bishop of Csanád in 1030. He lived during the reign of Stephen I and it was the king himself who summoned Gellért from the Benedictine Sant Giorgio Monastery in Venice to tutor the heir to the throne, Prince Imre. Gellért's influence was confirmed by the conversion of many pagans to Christianity. The pagan revolt which followed the death of Stephen in 1038 led to Gellért's martyrdom in 1046. According to the legend, he was thrown from the top of the hill inside a barrel. Canonised in 1083, Saint Gellért is a revered figure in Hungarian history.

The monumental bronze statue (by Gyula Jankovits, 1904) stands in a striking position on the place of his martyrdom, halfway down the hill in front of a semi-circular stone colonnade. Gellért, who seems to be blessing the city, holds a cross in his raised right hand. A converted pagan is represented at his feet. There is another fine **view★★** from here.

RUDAS BATHS★★

(Rudas Gyógyfürdő)

D7 – *Döbrentei tér, 9 – bus 5, 7, 8 Rudas Gyógyfürdő;* 🚊 *19, 41, 56, 56A Rudas Gyógyfürdő –* ♿ *p. 106.* There is nothing particularly special about this building from the outside; it was built in 1556 by the pasha Sokoli Mustafa. But inside it's a different story. A large octagonal marble pool is surrounded by eight columns supporting a rounded dome pierced by oculi through which coloured rays of light enter to dance upon the water. At each corner is a small pool with temperatures ranging from cold to hot. There's also a rooftop pool.

Gellért Baths

Víziváros★

(Watertown)

Part of Buda, this district sits below the castle and was known as 'water town' in the Middle Ages, due to the numerous thermal springs here.

▶**Access:** Ⓜ 2 Batthyány tér; to get here on foot from Pest, take the Chain Bridge (accessible from the Pest side from Ⓜ 1, 2 or 3 Deák Ferenc tér).
Detachable map C3–5.
♿ *Addresses p. 84, 90, 101 and 108.*

CHAIN BRIDGE★★

(Széchenyi Lánchíd)

C5 The oldest bridge in the city, the Chain Bridge is also known as Széchenyi Bridge, after the great Hungarian statesman Count István Széchenyi, who commissioned its construction. It has become one of the symbols of the city, if not *the* symbol. Arriving in Pest in December 1820, having learned of the death of his father, the young aristocrat and hussar captain found himself unable to take the ferry across the Danube due to ice having brought all river traffic to a standstill. Stuck in Pest for several days, the idea of building a bridge started to grow in his mind. Among the several designs proposed, the one by British engineers William Tierney Clark and Adam Clark was selected. The building work took place between 1839 and 1849 and the result was the first permanant stone crossing between Buda and Pest, with a span of 380m and width

The Danube

The second longest river in Europe after the Volga in Russia, the Danube (Duna in Hungarian) rises in the Black Forest in Germany and flows an astonishing 2,850km to the Black Sea. It wends its way across Hungary for one seventh of its length (428km). A number of the Danube's tributaries also flow across Hungary, like the Tisza, that rises in Ukraine, and the Drava with its source in northern Italy. The Drava also forms the the the border between Hungary and Croatia for some 150km. Most of the other tributaries flowing across Hungary, such as the Váli-víz and Sió, join the Danube's right bank. The Danube is a shallow river with an average depth of just 3 to 4m, and an average width of between 300m and 600m. It has been a vital means of transport and communication between the eastern and western countries of Europe since the Middle Ages. In 1992 the opening of the canal connecting the Danube to the rivers Main and Rhine created a new river route connecting the North Sea to the Black Sea.

Lions without tongues?

There is a strange story surrounding the four lions of the Chain Bridge that ends with the death of the sculptor. According to the legend, the lions of the Chain Bridge cannot speak because they have no tongues – the sculptor János Marchalkó forgot to give them tongues. The story goes that he felt so ashamed when everybody started to make fun of him for this oversight that he committed suicide by throwing himself in the Danube. In reality, Marchalkó did not commit suicide and the lions do in fact possess tongues, it is just that they are so small that you have to climb up and peer into their mouths to see them.

of 15.7m. The use of stone and iron creates a beautiful classical effect. Lit up at night, the suspension cables between the two pillars shaped like triumphal arches look like garlands of light. Two stone lions stand guard proudly at either end of the bridge, seated on pedestals. The bridge was blown up in 1945 during the Siege of Budapest, leaving only the pillars, but was rebuilt and reopened in 1949.

CLARK ÁDÁM TÉR

(Ádám Clark Square)
C5 – Tram *19, 41 Clark Ádám tér.*
The square has turned into a particularly busy large roundabout for the thousands of cars that emerge from or disappear into the tunnel under Buda Castle, the oldest tunnel in the city. The tunnel was designed and built by **Adam Clark** (1811–1866), the Scottish civil engineer who was also in charge of the construction of the Chain Bridge. Clark married Hungarian aristocrat Mária Áldásy and is buried in Kerepesi Cemetery. On the left you can see the sculpture marking **kilometre zero**, the point from which all road distances from the Hungarian capital are calculated.

FŐ UTCA

(Fő Street)
C3–4 The principal street in Víziváros, lined with various buildings, runs parallel to the Danube. At one time it was one of Buda's most important streets (Fő utca means 'Main Street'), and was bustling with merchants during the 18C. Nobel prize-winning biophysicst **Georg von Békésy** (1899–1972) lived at **no. 19**. The Pavillon de Paris French restaurant occupies **no. 20**. At **nos. 30** and **32** you can see the former Capuchin convent and its **church** before arriving at **Corvin tér**, which is home to several baroque houses (nos. 2 to 5). On the north side of the square is a stately neoclassical-style theatre building, the newly restored **Budai Vigadó** (not to be confused with Pesti Vigadó over the river in Pest on Vigadó tér), where the Hungarian State Folk Ensemble (Magyar Állami Népi Együttes) perform. Inside the building, dating from the late 1800s, are stone pillars and marble staircases and a 301-seat theatre with an Art Nouveau flavour Further along on the right you can see the red-brick neo-Gothic **Calvinist church** with a tall slender steeple and roof of Zsolnay tiles.

BATTHYÁNY TÉR

(Batthyány Square)
C3 – 🅜 *2 Batthyány tér.*
The square is also a useful public transport hub (metro line 2, bus, trams, HÉV commuter train line). It is named after **Count Lajos Batthyány** (1806–1849), a liberal politician who supported a compromise with Austria and led the first Hungarian government in 1848. He stepped down from his position following a disagreement with Lajos Kossuth, the leader of the liberal movement during the 1848–49 Hungarian Revolution, and was executed by the Austrians after the revolt failed.

The elegant baroque **Church of Saint Anne★ (Szent Anna templom)** dominates the square with its two identical bell towers and was built in the mid 18C. Above the entrance are allegorical statues of Faith, Hope and Charity. In the middle of the façade is a statue of Saint Anne with Mary. The interior is extravagantly decorated, in typical baroque style, notably including the high altar framed with marble columns, the dome's frescoes representing the Trinity, the gilded pulpit adorned with cherubs, and the organ casing. Somewhat delapidated after 200 years of wear and tear, the church was restored in the 1970s. Close by is **Angelika Restaurant and Café** (♿ *p. 90*), in what was once the church storehouse. It was often frequented by artist and writers and is today a nice place to stop and enjoy a cake, with a **view** of the Parliament Building on the opposite bank.

At **no. 3**, near the 19C **market halls**, is the former **White Cross Inn**, established around 1770. The building is distinguished by its reliefs representing the four seasons and its two wrought-iron balconies on either side of the main building, rococo in style on the right and baroque on the left. The entrance is through a door beneath street level. The 'Casanova Pub' sign is a reminder that the famous seducer is supposed to have passed this way during his tour of Europe at the end of the 18C.

On the north side of Nagy Imre tér, an austere and forbidding red-brick building occupying a full block is the **former Military Court of Justice**. It was used as a headquarters and prison by the Gestapo in 1944 and as the Fő Utca Prison, when it was the place of incarceration and torture of many victims of the Communist regime. Imre Nagy, leader of the 1956 Revolution, was imprisoned here before his execution.

KIRÁLY BATHS★★

(Király Gyógyfürdő)
C3 – Fő utca 82–84 – 🅜 *2 Batthyány tér* – 🚋 *19, 41 Bem József tér;* 🚌 *109 Bem József tér* – ♿ *p. 106.*
One of the oldest of Budapest's bath houses, built in 1565 by Arslan, pasha of Buda. Set back from Fő utca, the baths are now mixed and could do with a little refurbishment but are not so busy as some and there's certainly no lack of atmosphere. You can still see the original octagonal Ottoman bath beneath the green-domed roof.

Chain Bridge, Gresham Palace and St Stephen's Basilica in the background

Lipótváros★★★

(Leopold Town)

Budapest's political and administrative centre, the district of Lipótváros is named after Leopold II, king of Hungary, who reigned from 1790 to 1792. Along with Belváros, it forms part of the historical heart of Pest. Its monuments, tree-filled squares and antique shops along Falk Miksa utca make the neighbourhood a pleasure to explore on foot.

▶**Access:** Ⓜ 2 Kossuth Lajos tér; ⬛ 2 Kossuth Lajos tér.
Detachable map CD 3–5.
♿ *Addresses p. 84, 92, 94, 101 and 108.*

PARLIAMENT BUILDING★★★

(Országház)

C3 - Kossuth Lajos tér 1–3 - Ⓜ 2 Kossuth Lajos tér - ℘ (1) 441 4904 - latogatokozpont.parlament.hu - Same day tickets can be bought at the visitor centre, to the right of the Parliament Building, by the small museum (access on the lower floor), but the transaction can take a long time and visitor numbers are subject to a quota. Visitor centre open Apr–Oct 8am–6pm, Nov–Mar 8am–4pm. Visit by guided tour only, no tours during plenary sessions and public holidays. Ft3,500 EU citizens on presentation of ID, Ft6,700 non-Eu citizens. Tours in English daily at 10am, midday, 1pm. 2pm, 3pm.
☺ *Buying tickets in advance online is recommended, via: www.jegymester.hu/parlament (charge of Ft200 commission to collect tickets on site).*
A vast, very grand structure with the air of a neo-Gothic cathedral. Seen from across the Danube, the arcaded colonnades of the Parliament Building make it a striking landmark. With its dome, clock towers, pinnacles, spires, and galleries in Gothic revival style there's a hint of the British Houses of Parliament or even Milan's cathedral. It was built between 1885 and 1902 to plans drawn up by Imre Steindl. The parliamentary assembly first sat here in 1896 to mark the one thousandth anniversary of Hungary's foundation. Set into the façades are 88 solemn statues representing Hungarian sovereigns and military leaders.
Two symmetrical wings on either side meet under the dome. They were built when the parliament was divided into two houses, a house of representatives and an upper house. Today, the Parliament Building is the seat of the president of the Hungarian Republic (south wing), the government (north wing) and the national assembly.
The main entrance on Kossuth Lajos tér is decorated with stone lions and leads to the magnificent Grand Stairway (96 steps).

Interior – *The guided tour only covers one part of the building.* Sumptuous and awe-inspiring ... these are the kinds of words you will be grasping for on seeing the **Grand Stairway** and entrance hall, which are further enhanced by an abundance of gilding. On the ribbed vaulted ceiling are frescoes by Károly Lotz, *The Apotheosis of Legislation* and *The Glorification of Hungary.*

The **Dome Hall**, an immense circular room, contains statues of successive sovereigns and the coats of arms of the old Hungarian counties. Also on display are the **crown jewels★★**. They were transferred here from the National Museum to mark the the millennial of the coronation of Stephen I. The **Holy Crown** was returned to Hungary by the Americans in 1978 – at the end of the Second World War it was placed for safekeeping (from the Russians) in the United States (in Fort Knox). Also known as the Crown of Saint Stephen and bearing Hungary's coat of arms, it is a magnificent example of gold metalwork, probably created in the 11C. Its Byzantine lower section, the 'Greek Crown' is made up of cloisonné enamel plaques, set with precious stones and representing saints and archangels. Byzantine emperor Michael VII Doukas is portrayed in the centre. The upper 'Latin Crown' consists of two plaques of gold and enamel crossed over each other, bearing a Christ in Majesty and portraits of two apostles whose names are inscribed in Latin. The cross on the top is crooked (damaged over the years). The **Sceptre** in silver and rock crystal has both Egyptian and Hungarian origins. The **Orb**, topped with the patriarchal cross and struck with the arms of the House of Anjou, dates back to the 14C (the reign of Charles I of Hungary). The **Sword** was produced by a 16C Venetian workshop. The statues in the **Lounge of the Chamber of Peers** are allegories of the trades of commerce and industry. The **Chamber of Peers** is lined in oak. It is here that the president directs debates in front of the parliamentary members on seating arranged in a horseshoe shape. In the corridors you can see seats reserved for members of the chamber with numbered cigar holders (each corresponding to a parliamentarian).

SHOES ON THE DANUBE BANK

C4 – *Id Antall József rkp.*
On the riverbank, to the right of the Parliament Building, is a line of sixty pairs of shoes cast in metal. They commemorate the massacre of thousands of Jews during the Second World War by the terrible Arrow Cross party (👁 *p. 62*). The executions often took place on the river bank where the Jews were made to remove their shoes before being shot and their bodies thrown into the Danube.

HOUSE OF HUNGARIAN ART NOUVEAU★

(Magyar Szecesszió Háza)
D3 – *Honvéd utca 3* – 🅜 *2 Kossuth Lajos tér or 3 Arany János utca;* 🚋 *2 Kossuth Lajos tér* – ☎ *(1) 269*

46 22 – www.magyarszecessziohaza. hu – 10am–5pm – closed Sun – Ft2,000.

The purpose of this museum is to highlight the unique way Art Nouveau developed into the Secessionst style in Hungary (♿ *p. 129)*. It occupies the Bedő family's house, a jewel of Art Nouveau architecture built in 1903 by the Secessionist architect Emil Vidor. Painting, furniture and decorative objects jostle for space over three floors; it's almost more like an antique shop than a museum. Dedicated museum visitors may bemoan the less than strict museography but the museum recreates the atmosphere of the period very successfully.

SZABADSÁG TÉR★

(Liberty Square)

D4 – Ⓜ *3 Arany János utca.*

On the site of a former Austrian barracks, this large public square is lined with buildings with grand façades, such as the **National Bank of Hungary (Magyar Nemzeti Bank)** and, opposite, the old Stock Exchange, a building that for a time was the home of the **State Television** studios and is now undergoing refurbishment, transforming it into high-end offices and shops. Both buildings are the work of the architect Ignác Alpár.

On the south side of the square the erection of the **Monument to the Victims of the German Occupation (A német megszállás áldozatainak emlékműve)** in 2014 has proved controversial. It shows the German Imperial eagle attacking Hungary, portrayed as the Archangel Gabriel. To its detractors it represents a 'falsification of history' because it is seen as minimizing the country's responsibility in the deportation of Jews and Romanis.

Surrounded by lawns and to the north of the square, is the only monument in Budapest dedicated to the Soviets, the **Monument to the Soviet Red Army**, which takes the form of an obelisk. They liberated the city from the Germans in 1945. The **United States Embassy** is also here in the square, along with a **statue** of **General Harry Hill Bandholtz**. After the fall of the Republic of Councils in 1919, he reportedly held off Romanian looters intent on taking treasures from the National Museum armed solely with a riding crop and the sheer force of his personality.

POSTAL SAVINGS BANK★★

(Posta Takarékpénztár)

D4 – *Hold utca 4* – Ⓜ *3 Arany János utca; bus 15, 115 Hold utca.*

The decoration of this building (1901) by **Ödön Lechner** (♿ *p. 130)* is quite dazzling. From the elegant façade to the highly ornate roof, it is a mix of mosaics and ceramics and is now home to the offices of the Treasury.

DOWNTOWN MARKET

(Belvárosi Piac)

D3–4 – *Hold utca 13* – Ⓜ *3 Arany János utca* – *6.30am–6pm (Mon 5pm, Fri 10pm, Sat 4pm) – closed Sun.*

A food market worth the detour for its stands and its metal work

Detail of Postal Savings Bank building

architecture. Upstairs there are several very decent cafeteria-style eateries.

BUDAPEST–NYUGATI RAILWAY TERMINAL★

(Nyugati Pályaudvar)
E2–3 – Ⓜ *3 and* 🚊 *4, 6 Nyugati pályaudvar.*
Opened in 1877, it was built by the Eiffel company of Eiffel Tower fame and is one of Budapest's three main railway terminals. An artful combination of steel, glass and brick, its large glass-fronted forecourt opens onto Baross tér. While you might not be able to see the ornate private waiting room of Emperor Franz Joseph I, the ticket office hall demonstrates the building's old-school grandeur very well.

ST STEPHEN'S BASILICA★★

(Szent István Bazilika)
D4 – *Szent István tér –* Ⓜ *1 Bajcsy-Zslinszka. út or* Ⓜ *1 and 2 Deák Ferenc tér – www.bazilika.biz – 9am–5pm, Sat 9am–1pm, Sun 1pm–5pm – free – for the concert programme see en.bazilika.biz/.*
The basilica was constructed between 1851 and 1906, and was inaugurated by Emperor Franz Joseph I. Architect József Hild bagan the work, which was continued after his death in 1867 by Miklós Ybl. It was Ybl who gave the basilica its monumental aspect in a neo-Renaissance style,

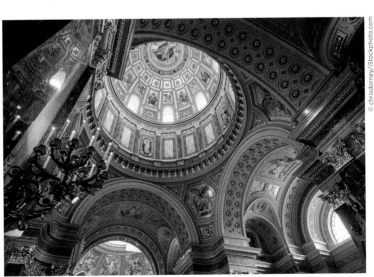

© chrisdorney/iStockphoto.com

Interior, St Stephen's Basilica

and it has become one of the most photographed sites in the city, gloriously illuminated at night. In the centre of the relatively austere façade look for an archway with a sculpted pediment showing the Virgin surrounded by Hungarian saints. Craning your neck, high up you can also see superb statues by Leó Fessler: the Four Evangelists (base of the dome), the Church Fathers (towers), the Twelve Apostles (apse – *walk around the building via the right-hand side*). The decoration of the interior, laid out in the shape of a Greek cross, is sumptuous with gilding and marble decoration. The interior of the dome (height 96m) is decorated with mosaics. On the high altar is a statue of Saint Stephen in Carrara marble with bas-reliefs depicting scenes from his life. The **Chapel of the Holy Dexter** *(to the left of the choir)* displays one of the church's showpieces – the mummified right hand (the Holy Dexter) of Saint Stephen, who was also Stephen I, the first king of Hungary, canonised in 1083. It is carried in procession on 20 August, St Stephen's Day.
North Tower (Körpanoráma) – *10am–4.30pm (6.30pm in summer)* – Ft600. Beautiful **panoramic view★★**.

GRESHAM PALACE★

(Gresham palota)
D5 – *Széchenyi tér 5–6* – 🚊 *2 Eötvös tér.*
Another example of the Secessionist style (1907), this is one of the most significant buildings in the city. It is named after the London-based insurance company that bought the building in 1880. The company was itself named after the founder of the London Stock Exchange (the Royal Exchange), Thomas Gresham (1519–1579), who was a financial advisor to the English Crown. It has since been used as a Red Army barracks, an apartment building and is today the home of a luxury hotel. The façade looking over Széchenyi tér is decorated with sculpted stone reliefs. Between the two world wars, the Gresham Café was a popular meeting place for artists.

HUNGARIAN ACADEMY OF SCIENCES

(Magyar Tudományos Akadémia)
D4 – *Széchenyi tér 9* – 🚊 *2 Eötvös tér.*
This is one of the most beautiful examples of a 19C neo-Renaissance building. During the first Diet (legislative assembly) of 1825–1827, Count István Széchenyi offered a year's income from his estate to build this academy. On the top floor, the six statues represent the six main departments: law, science, mathematics, philosophy, linguistics and history. On the façade facing the Danube are allegorical statues: Archaeology, Poetry, Astronomy, and Political Science. At the corners of the building look out for statues of several eminent figures from history: Sir Isaac Newton, Russian polymath Lomonosov, Galileo, Hungarian linguist and writer Révay, French philopsopher Descartes and German mathematician Leibniz.

Andrássy út★★

(Andrássy Avenue)

The most elegant avenue in the capital has on occasion been called the 'Champs-Élysées of Budapest', and it does indeed contain some of the most beautiful examples of Budapest's architecture, with buildings decorated with mosaics, statues and friezes. Many house upmarket shops, along with theatres, the Opera House and both the Liszt and Kodály museums. Andrássy út begins as a lively and busy thoroughfare before turning into a residential area beyond Kodály Körönd. You will see apartment blocks and old buildings with façades decorated with sculptures, alongside beautiful villas and extremely plush hotels. Many foreign embassies are also located here.

▶**Access:** Ⓜ line 1; one of the first metro lines in service in Europe (1896). Despite its age it works perfectly and you can be transported from the city centre to City Park in just 10min. Bus no. 105 runs the length of Andrássy út.
Detachable map E 3–4, F 2–3, G2.
🍴 *Addresses p. 85, 92, 96 & 101.*

44

STATE OPERA HOUSE★★

(Magyar Állami Operaház)
*E4 – Andrássy út 22 – Ⓜ 1 Opera.
📞 (30) 279 5677 – www.operavisit.hu
– reconstruction works until 2020, guided tour in English daily at 3pm & 4pm of the rooms that are open – Ft2,490 (including 'mini' concert).*
This neo-Renaissance opera house was built between 1875 and 1884 by Miklós Ybl. The façade features a porch entrance with a loggia above. Two niches on either side of the entrance contain statues of two great Hungarian composers: to the right, **Franz Liszt** (1811–1886) and to the left, **Ferenc Erkel** (1810–1893). Erkel, who was born in Gyula and died in Budapest, was both a pianist and a talented conductor.

Having written the national anthem as well as several operas, he also conducted the concert at the grand opening of the Opera House in September 1884, when the overture of his opera *Hunyadi László* was played, in addition to other pieces. The upper section of the building is decorated with a balustrade topped with statues of famous composers (Mozart, Beethoven, Rossini, Wagner, Bizet, Smetana...). The **interior** is sumptuous, with a great staircase, a foyer, a 'smoker's corridor', the auditorium (with frescoes by Károly Lotz depicting the *Apotheosis of Music* on the ceiling), a reception room and the royal staircase, resplendent with gilt, wood panelling, frescoes, paintings and marble carvings.

State Opera House

NEW THEATRE★

(Új Színház)
E4 – Paulay Ede utca 35 – Ⓜ *1 Opera.*
Set slightly set back from Andrássy út, the New Theatre is a masterful reconstruction (1990) of the beautiful and intimate building envisioned by Béla Lajta (1909). Above the entrance nine gilt ceramic angels, each holding a blue plaque, spell out the name of the theatre. The interior (a fine example of early Art Deco) is even more fascinating, with a harmonious colour scheme blending cream and blue alongside metallic grills, sleek curves, mirrors, and chromed light fittings. The theatre specialises in Hungarian drama in repertory.

HUNGARIAN HOUSE OF PHOTOGRAPHY★

(Magyar Fotográfusok Háza)
E4 – Nagymező utca 20 – Ⓜ *1 Opera –*
✆ *(30) 505 0455 – maimano.hu –*
midday-7pm – closed Mon & public holidays – Ft1,500 (free with the Budapest Card).
The building that was once home to the great Hungarian photographer **Mai Manó** (1855–1917) and his photographic studio now houses a photography museum in the heart of the theatre district. Temporary exhibitions by photographers from Hungary and further afield are held in this charming spot that dates back to the turn of the 19C. You will find a luxurious staircase with an iron balustrade, frescoes, stucco, stained glass windows by Miksa Ráth, and a studio lit by a skylight. The view onto

the Operetta Theatre opposite will take you back to Mai Manó's day.

ROBERT CAPA CONTEMPORARY PHOTOGRAPHY CENTRE

(Robert Capa Kortárs Fotográfiai Központ)
E4 – Nagymező utca 8 – Ⓜ *Opera –*
✆ *(1) 413 1310 – capacenter.hu –*
11am-7pm – Ft1,500 (free with the Budapest Card).
Opened in 2013 in the former Ernst Museum, this centre is further evidence of the Hungarian fascination with photography. Its name pays homage to the famous Hungarian war photographer and photojournalist **Robert Capa** (1913–1954). Capa risked his life numerous times covering the major wars of the mid-20C, including the Spanish Civil War and the Second World War. The centre is the contemporary counterpart to the Hungarian House of Photography and holds regular temporary exhibitions.

PARIS DEPARTMENT STORE

(Párisi Nagy Áruház)
E4 – Andrássy út 39 – Ⓜ *1 Opera or Oktogon.*
The high society of yesteryear once formed the clientele of the store that lurks behind this grand Art Deco façade. Until 2017 the building housed the Alexandra Bookstore and a teashop in its magnificent Lotz ballroom, but this is now occupied by the Café Parisi, while on the roof the **360 Bar** (🍸 *p. 102*) is a watering-hole with a panoramic view, just as it was back in 1911.

© Sergio Delle Vedove/iStockphoto.com

Terror Háza

LISZT FERENC TÉR

E4 – **M** *1 Oktogon* – **Tram** *4, 6 Oktogon.*
This shady **square** with a small
garden in the centre has become
a focal point for this area devoted
to the performing arts. With cafés,
restaurants and jazz clubs finding
a home here, it's a popular spot for
Budapesters to meet with friends and
check out the latest 'hot show'.

FRANZ LISZT ACADEMY OF MUSIC

**(Liszt Ferenc Zeneművészeti
Főiskola)**
E4 – *Liszt Ferenc tér 8* – **M** *1 Oktogon*
– **Tram** *4, 6 Oktogon.*
This academy was founded by the
eponymous famous composer and

his bronze statue, crafted by Alajos
Stróbl, adorns the façade. The
opulently appointed **foyer★** (entrance
on Király utca) is a small Art Nouveau
gem, with gilt mosaics reminiscent
of Klimt, metallic cartouches, green
earthenware tiles and a fountain, not
to mention some perfectly preserved
locker rooms. An extensive renovation
of the building was completed in 2013.

HOUSE OF TERROR MUSEUM★★

(Terror Háza)
E3 – *Andrássy út 60* –
M *1 Vörösmarty utca* – **Tram** *4,
6 Oktogon* – ✆ *(1) 374 2600* –
www.terrorhaza.hu – *10am–6pm* –
closed Mon & public holidays –
Ft3,000. Not suitable for children.

As a place of remembrance the museum is unique. It is unflinching in the way it faces up to the dark underside of dictatorship, and many Hungarians are still wary of visiting. In 1944 the building, along with several others in the area, was used as the general headquarters of the Hungarian Nazi party, the feared Arrow Cross Party, and in 1956 it became the nerve centre of the ÁVO and the ÀVH, the Communist state police.

The exhibition begins on the second floor and the suffering experienced here becomes palpable as effective stagecraft (propaganda posters, uniforms, films, recorded sound, witness accounts, use of light and shadow, the personal effects of victims...) is used to movingly evoke those dark years. With reconstructions of a train used for deportations and a wiretapping room, we become visitors to a crime scene and the exhibition is set up to powerfully recreate the atmosphere of the period.

Next is a slow descent by lift to the basement, watching a film in which a torturer explains (with subtitles in English) what he was expected to do. The reconstructed torture chambers leave little to the imagination and leave a lasting impression on many visitors. The last room shows amateur footage of the departure of the Russian army. It is interesting to note the almost childlike faces of the Russian solders, who seem to have allowed events go over their heads, with little idea of why they were there, or why they are leaving.

FRANZ LISZT MUSEUM★

(Liszt Ferenc Emlékmúzeum)
F3 – *Vörösmarty utca 35* –
Ⓜ *1 Vörösmarty utca.* ✆ *(1) 322 9804 – www.lisztmuseum.hu – Mon–Fri 10am–6pm, Sat 9am–5pm – closed Sun & public holidays*, Dec 26 & 30 – Ft2,000 – audioguide in English Ft700.

The apartment in which **Franz Liszt** spent the winter during the last five years of his life consists of three rooms. It records the life of an artist who by then had achieved great fame. The bedroom, office and performance room still contain personal effects (tuning forks, spectacles, letters, a hat, a walking stick, a rosary, a prayer book that was a gift from the pope). The Bösendorfer piano in the sitting room was the artist's favourite instrument. A concert is given at 11am every Saturday *(included in the price of the ticket)*.

KODÁLY KÖRÖND

(Kodály Circus)
F3 – Ⓜ *1 Kodály körönd.*
This elegant circus is ringed by four symmetrical buildings and features statues of four Hungarian heroes shown defending the kingdom.

ZOLTÁN KODÁLY MUSEUM

(Kodály Zoltán Emlékmúzeum)
F3 – *Andrássy út 89* – Ⓜ *1 Kodály körönd* – ✆ *(1) 352 7106 – kodaly.hu/ museum – Wed–Fri 10am–midday, 2pm–4.30pm, visit by appointment only – closed Aug – Ft1,500.*

Along with Béla Bartók, **Zoltán Kodály** (👟 *p. 133*) had a great influence on 20C Hungarian music. The apartment he lived in from March 1924 until his death in March 1967 contains numerous effects belonging to this great composer: pianos, a library full of books, a writing desk and manuscript scores. You will also learn about a little-known side to his talents – he was a keen potter (a collection of pots is exhibited in the dining room).

FERENC HOPP MUSEUM OF ASIATIC ARTS

(Hopp Ferenc Kelet–Ázsiai Művészeti Múzeum)
F2 – Andrássy út 103 – 🅼 *1 Bajza utca* – 🖉 *(1) 469 7762* – *hoppmuseum.hu* – *Daily 10am–6pm, closed Mon* – *Ft1,200 (free with the Budapest Card) – guided tour available, groups of up to 15 Ft10,000 per group.*
Ferenc Hopp (1833–1919), an optician and one of the country's great travellers, donated to his homeland the objects he gathered on his many expeditions to Asia. The museum, which has been housed in his former villa since 1923, displays the items on rotation, along with acquisitions from other sources.

VÁROSLIGETI FASOR

(Városliget Boulevard)
FG3 – 🅼 *1 Bajza utca.*
This tree-lined residential street contains a number of beautiful Art Nouveau villas and provides an alternative route to Andrássy út on your return to City Park (Városliget, 👟 *p. 50*). When you reach the park, which is opposite Városligeti street, don't forget to look at the **Memorial to the 1956 Hungarian Revolution** erected in 2006 on the 50th anniversary of the uprising and abstract in style.

GYÖRGY RÁTH MUSEUM★

(Ráth György Múzeum)
F3 – Városligeti fasor 12 – 🅼 *1 Bajza utca* – 🖉 *(1) 416 9601* – *www.imm.hu* – *Daily 10am–6pm, closed Mon* – *Ft2,000 (reduced price with the Budapest Card).*
Bought in 1901 by György Ráth, the first director of the Museum of Applied Arts, this villa opened its doors as a museum in 2018. Having once served as an annex to the Ferenc Hopp Museum (next door), it now displays exhibits from the Art Nouveau collection belonging to the Museum of Applied Arts (👟 *p. 66*).

ING BANK BUILDING

G2 – Dózsa György út 84b – 🅼 *1 Bajza utca or Hősök tere.*
It is impossible not to have a view on the ING bank headquarters designed by Dutch architect Erick Van Egeraat and it has become something of a landmark in the city. The reflective glass and steel façade gives the impression of a building in a constant state of flux and it looks different depending on the light and the angle from which you are viewing it.

49

Városliget★★
(City Park)

Városliget is the city's largest park and, like Margitsziget (Margaret Island), is very popular with Budapesters and tourists alike, especially during the summer. Families come here looking for a shady spot in the hot weather, to wander along its many paths and enjoy a visit to some of the best baths in Budapest or perhaps to go skating in winter. By 2021 the massive Liget restoration project should be finished and Kós Károly sétány, the road that crosses the park, will be closed to traffic. Pedestrian paths are being revamped, cycle paths opened and picnic areas installed. There will be an illuminated jogging track and other sports facilities. Play areas for children are being spruced up and the zoo extended. Despite all this outdoor activity, culture is not neglected, with a theatre, the Museum of Ethnography and the new National Gallery due to open in the park.

▶**Access:** Ⓜ 1 Hősök tere. ***Detachable map FGH 1-3.***
▶**Tip:** For information about the redesign of the park, see ligetbudapest.hu.
Ⓖ *Addresses p. 86.*

HŐSÖK TERE

(Heroes' Square)

G2 Flanked to the left by the Museum of Fine Arts and to the right by the Hall of Art, Heroes' Square was designed by the architect Albert Schickedanz. Over the years it has become a major rallying and assembly point for mass demonstrations and public celebrations. At its centre, a tall column (36m) topped with a statue of the Archangel Gabriel surveys the people coming and going across the square below. The angel stands on a globe that bears the Hungarian crown and an apostolic cross. An impressive group of sculptures is arranged around the plinth below depicting the Magyar prince Árpád seated on a horse, accompanied by six other Hungarian tribal chiefs. Behind the column is the **Millennium Monument ★ (Millenniumi emlékmű)**, consisting of two colonnades arranged in an arc, flanking a collection of statues and sculptures. As its name suggests, the monument commemorates the thousandth anniversary of the Hungarian conquest and work on it began in 1896. The colonnade is divided into two symmetrical sections, at the top of which there are allegorical statues representing Labour and Wealth (on the left) and Knowledge and Glory (on the right); these stand opposite the chariots of War and of Peace.
Interspersed between the columns are statues of historical figures (kings and princes) who have left a major mark on the history of the country.

Millennium Monument and the column with the statue of the Archangel Gabriel, Heroes' Square

They include Stephen I, Béla IV, Louis the Great, Matthias Corvinus, several princes of Transylvania, Gabriel Bethlen and Francis II Rákóczi. There is also one man of the people, Lajos Kossuth, a hero of the 1848 Revolution. Beneath each of these is a relief sculpture depicting a scene from the life of the character in question.

MUSEUM OF FINE ARTS★★★

(Szépművészeti Múzeum)
FG 1–2 – Dózsa György út 41 (Hősök tere) – Ⓜ *1 Hősök tere – ✆ (1) 469 7100 – www.szepmuveszeti.hu – Tue–Sun 10am–5.30pm, closed Mon – permanent collection Ft2,000 (free with the Budapest Card), permanent collection & temporary exhibition Ft3,000, audioguide in English Ft800. ♿ Art post 1800 is on display at the Hungarian National Gallery (♿ p. 17).*
This museum is renowned for its collection of paintings and features an entrance that is a worthy match for the magnificence of its exhibits. You enter through a colossal portico of eight Greek-inspired Corinthian columns (the pediment is a replica of the one on top of the Temple of Zeus at Olympia). The museum's historic halls have been restored, including some that had long been closed but are now reopened. Hence it has been possible to return to the museum the collection of Old Hungarian Masters (from the Middle Ages to the end of the 18C), which was at one time exhibited at the National Gallery. It contains a beautiful **collection of altarpieces**★ in particular. A feature of altarpiece art, which flourished

from the 15C to the beginning of the 16C are triptychs and polyptychs, and there are some huge examples here from the old Hungarian counties of Szepes (Szepes altar), Sáros (Mary Magdalene altar), Liptó (altar of St Andrew) and Csík (high altar of the Descent of the Holy Spirit).
The great European schools of painting from the 13C to the 18C are also represented, providing a panorama of the top names from art history. In February 2019 the museum unveiled its newly purchased *Portrait of Princess Mary* (eldest daughter of King Charles I of England) by **Sir Anthony van Dyck**, painted in 1641, bought at Christie's in London.
Italian painting (1250–1800) – the Quattrocento (15C), with works by Domenico Ghirlandaio (*Saint Stephen*) and Gentile Bellini (*Portrait of Caterina Cornaro, Queen of Cyprus*). The following century, the Cinquecento, is represented by works from Leonardo da Vinci (an equestrian statue attributed to him), Raphael, Titian (*Portrait of Doge Marcantonio Trevisani*), Veronese (*Portrait of a Man*) and Tintoretto. The baroque rooms feature works by Tiepolo, in particular.
French painting (1550–1800) – These include canvases by leading exponent of the baroque style Nicolas Poussin, as well as Claude Lorrain (*Villa in the Roman Countryside*, 1647), Eugène Delacroix (*Frightened Horse Leaving the Water*, 1825), Gustave Courbet (*Wrestlers*, 1853), Edouard Manet (*Woman with Fan*, 1862), Paul Cézanne (*The Buffet*, 1874), Claude Monet (*Three Fishing Boats*, 1885),

Museum of Fine Arts

Paul Gauguin (*The Black Pigs*, 1891). There are also several sculptures by Carpeaux, Rodin and Maillol.

German and Austrian painting (1400–1800) – Look out for a great work by Hans Holbein the Elder (*The Dormition of the Virgin*, 15C). The German Renaissance is represented by Dürer (*Portrait of a Young Man*) and Lucas Cranach the Elder.

Early Netherlandish painting – From the 16C, there is Hans Memling, Gerard David (*The Nativity*), and Pieter Bruegel the Elder.

Golden Age of Flemish Painting (1600–1800) – Masterpieces by Rubens, Van Dyck and Jordaens.

Spanish painting – Don't miss a Mary Magdalene and a darker picture, *The Agony in the Garden of Gethsemane*, by El Greco, or *The Lunch* by Velasquez. Goya's *Young Woman with a Pitcher* is another fine example of the genre. Works by Murillo (*The Infant Jesus Distributing Bread to Pilgrims*) and Jusepe de Ribera, who worked primarily in Italy and is famed for his lively realism, round off this school.

The **Egyptian art collection** contains some remarkable pieces, while other significant collections include **Greek and Roman relics** and **collections of 20C and contemporary art** (Victor Vasarely, Simon Hantaï, Pablo Picasso, among others), not to mention the section devoted to **European sculpture**.

HALL OF ART

(Műcsarnok/Kunsthalle)

G2 – *Dózsa György út 37 –* 🚇 *1 Hősök tere –* ☎ *(1) 460 7000 – www. mucsarnok.hu – Tue–Sun 10am–6pm, Thur midday–8pm – Ft1,800/2,900 depending on visit (free with the Budapest Card) – shop and café (daily except Mon, 10am–11pm).*

This building located opposite the Museum of Fine Arts looks rather like a Greek temple and holds temporary exhibitions only. An immense **statue of Stalin** (8m high) once stood nearby, behind the building. A major symbol of Soviet oppression, it was torn down and destroyed on the night of 23 October 1956. Nothing of it remains today, but you can see a replica of the statue's enormous boots, which are on display in Memento Park (♿ *p. 77*).

MUSEUM OF ETHNOGRAPHY

(Néprajzi Múzeum)

G2 – *www.neprajz.hu. The collection was originally crammed into the former royal court of cassation in the Lipótváros district, but closed in December 2017. It is scheduled to reopen in 2020 in a brand new building in Városliget.*

The ethnographic collection is particularly extensive. It provides a good insight into the region's rural communities, including exhibits from Upper Hungary (present-day Slovakia) and Transylvania (Romania) from the 18C to the turn of the 20C, the era before the Treaty of Trianon (1920), which decided the future of Hungary at the end of the First World War. It explores culture, fishing, handicrafts, fairgrounds and markets, the family and traditional festivals, all by means of photographs, folk art, costumes, tools and other various objects from everyday life.

ZOO & BOTANICAL GARDEN

(Állatkert)

F1 – *Állatkerti krt. 6-12 –* 🚇 *1 Széchenyi Fürdő –* ☎ *(1) 273 4900 – www.zoo budapest.com – May–Aug 9am–6pm (Fri–Sun 7pm), Apr & Sept 9am–5.30pm (Fri–Sun 6pm), Mar & Oct 9am–5pm (Fri–Sun 5.30pm), Jan–Feb & Nov–Dec 9am–4pm (24 & 31 Dec 1pm) – Ft3,000, children Ft2,000 (reduced prices with the Budapest Card).*

The zoo opened its doors in 1866 and is one of the oldest in the world. The entrance takes the form of a monumental gate flanked by two stone elephants. Once inside you will find more than 500 mammals, 700 birds, 1,500 reptiles and fish, along with a range of buildings and decorative elements characteristic of Budapest's Art Nouveau tradition. The elephant house looks like a palace from *One Thousand and One Nights*.

VAROSLIGET ICE RINK

(Városligeti Műjégpálya)

G2 – *Olof Palme sétány 5 –* 🚇 *1 Hősök tere –* ☎ *(1) 363 2673 – www.mujegpalya.hu – hours and ticket prices vary, see website.*

This 18,000sq m open-air skating rink (the largest in Europe) in City Park has been a favourite winter playground with the locals for years – it opened in 1926 and soon became an unmissable attraction. The lake that used to freeze over naturally is now transformed into a picturesque ice rink, floodlit at night. In spring it is transformed back into a lake again.

VAJDAHUNYAD CASTLE★

(Vajdahunyad vára)
G2 – 🚇 *1 Hősök tere or Széchenyi fürdő* – ✆ *(1) 422 0765* – *www. vajdahunyadcastle.com* – *courtyard accessible 24hr.*
The castle is an eclectic collection of architectural styles built for the 1896 Millennial Exhibition copying examples of landmark Hungarian buildings, which goes some way to explaining why you will find Roman, Gothic, Renaissance and baroque all rubbing shoulders with one another. The main building was inspired by Corvin Castle (formerly Vajdahunyad) in Transylvania (in present-day Romania). The courtyard of the castle is accessed via a bridge with three spans. Once inside, you will see **Ják Chapel** to the left. The gateway, with sculptures representing the twelve apostles, is reminiscent of the old Benedictine abbey church at Ják in west Hungary, which dates back to the 13C. Seated on a marble bench in front of the baroque part of the castle, his face hidden beneath a hood, you will find the strange figure of **Anonymus**, a scribe at the court of King Béla III (12C), represented in a bronze by Miklós Ligeti (1903). The castle houses the **Museum of Hungarian Agriculture** (**Magyar Mezőgazdasági Múzeum**) – *www.mezogazdasagimuzeum. hu* – *Oct–Apr 10am–5pm, Nov–Mar Tue–Fri 10am–4pm, weekends*

10am–5pm– closed Mon – Ft1,600). An exhibition on the history of land use, animal husbandry, fishing, hunting and viticulture *(signs in English)*.

SZÉCHENYI BATHS★★★

(Széchenyi Gyógyfürdő)
G1 – *Állatkerti krt. 11* – 🚇 *1 Széchenyi fürdő* – *szechenyispabaths.com* – ♿ *p. 106.*
Said to be one of the largest thermal spring complexes in Europe, its architecture is as opulent as you could possibly wish for, with an orgy of cherubs and statues. However you spend your day here, with your family, lounging about with friends, playing poolside chess, or paddling about in the dozen or so pools, there is something for everyone. Outside you will find a swimming pool, a large 'endless' pool (swim against the current), a hot tub (38°C), naturist areas and a restaurant. In winter, with snow covering the beaches and steam drifting about the complex, it is very atmospheric. Named after statesman István Széchenyi, the baths were opened in 1913 and are the deepest and warmest in the city (75°C).

MUNICIPAL GRAND CIRCUS

(Fővárosi Nagycirkusz)
G1 – *Állatkerti krt. 12/a* – 🚇 *1 Széchenyi fürdő* – ✆ *(1) 343 8300* – *www.fnc.hu* – *shows Wed–Fri 3pm; Sat 11am, 3pm & 7pm; Sun 11am & 3pm –Ft1,500/ 4,500 (children Ft1,500/3,150).*
Hungarian artists of international renown and circus troupes from overseas all appear here – acrobats, magic acts and circus specialities.

55

Belváros★★
(The City)

The name of this district means 'inner city or 'city centre' and Belváros and neighbouring Lipótváros make up the historic heart of Pest. Home to banks, government buildings, businesses, cafés and restaurants, Belváros is a very lively area during the day. A commercial hub, its many pedestrianised streets are ideal for shopping, while a stroll beside the river, when the traffic has died down in the evenings or on Sundays, is very pleasant.

▶**Access:** Ⓜ 3 or 4 Kálvin tér; 🚊 47, 49 Kálvin tér; bus 9, 15, 115 Kálvin tér.
Detachable map DE 5–7.
▶**Tip:** Stick to the smaller roads and pedestrianised streets as the large roads in the centre of Pest are often swamped with traffic.
◔ *Addresses p. 86, 92, 96, 102 and 109.*

METROPOLITAN ERVIN SZABÓ LIBRARY★

(Szabó Ervin könyvtár)
E6–7 – Szabó Ervin tér 1– Ⓜ 3, 4 Kálvin tér – ℘ (1) 411 5000 – www. fszek.hu – Mon-Fri 10am–8pm, Sat 10am–4pm – Ft1,000 (tourist ticket).
The Szabó Ervin Library is housed in three adjacent buildings. The main building is the **neo-baroque Wenckheim Palace**, whose extravagantly ornate exterior features impressive wrought-iron railings. It is a working library but visitors can buy an entrance ticket and take a look inside. Most head up to the 4th floor where you can see bedrooms, ballrooms and the former **smoking room**★ with beautiful wooden spiral staircases leading up to an ornate gallery. There's a café near the library entrance, which was once the palace stables.

HUNGARIAN NATIONAL MUSEUM★★

(Magyar Nemzeti Múzeum)
E6 – Múseum krt. 14–16 – Ⓜ 3, 4 Kálvin tér – ℘ (1) 338 2122 – mnm.hu – Daily except Mon 10am–6pm – Ft1,600 (free with the Budapest Card) – guided tour in English for up to 6 persons Ft8,000 + supplementary ticket per person Ft1,100.
Founded in 1802 by Count Ferenc Széchenyi, the museum is housed in a neoclassical palace fronted by a large portico of Corinthian columns. The carvings on the tympanum depict allegories of Pannonia (an ancient region of Central Europe corresponding to modern-day Hungary, and extending over parts of Croatia, Serbia, Bosnia-Herzegovina, Slovenia, Austria and Slovakia) surrounded by the Arts and Sciences. In front of the façade is a sculpture of

the great 19C Hungarian poet **János Arany** (1817–1882), while statues of other scholars, poets and politicians are scattered throughout the gardens surrounding the museum. On the ground floor, the coronation robes in purple Byzantine silks were a gift from King Stephen I and his queen to the Basilica of the Assumption of the Blessed Virgin Mary in Székesfehérvár, central Hunary, and are contemporay with the crown jewels on display in the Parliament Building. Rooms on the first floor depict significant moments from the country's history, from the arrival of the Magyar tribes to the post-Communist period. Each era is well illustrated with maps, plans, dioramas, films and artworks, along with other objects including weapons, furniture and clothes.

The extremely beautiful Gothic choirstalls in the room devoted to Matthias/Mátyás Hunyadi (Matthias Corvin) are from the basilica at Bártfa. In the next room (covering the Ottoman Occupation of the second half of the 16C), you'll find further choirstalls; these were taken from the Franciscan church at Nyírbátor and are a masterpiece of Hungarian cabinetmaking of the period. Note the intricacy of the detailing and the way the artists have created what looks like lacework out of wood. Also, look out for a ceramic coffered ceiling in the room covering the expulsion of the Turks. The rooms covering the modern era (20C) show the role played – and indeed the suffering endured – by Hungary under the rule of dictators, including: Miklós Horthy,

who had an ambivalent attitude towards Hitler's Germany and gave free reign to the sinister Arrow Cross Party, the Hungarian Nazis; Mátyás Rákosi, the Communist prime minister who orchestrated the 'red terror' of the 1950s involving the imprisonment and murder of thousands. This was followed by the 1956 Revolution, and finally the downfall of Communisim and the proclamation of the new Hungarian Republic and a new constitution on 23 October 1989.

FRANCISCAN CHURCH★

Ferences templom
D6 – *Ferenciek tere 2* – Ⓜ *3 Ferenciek tere.*
The entrance is via a porch framed by columns and topped with the arms of the Franciscan Order. The façade features three niches housing statues of St Peter of Alcantara, St Anthony of Padua and St Francis of Assisi. The interior is very ornate, with a central aisle but no side aisles. **Franz Liszt** used to hear mass here – there is a marker on one pew to show his habitual seat. The ceiling frescoes are themed around the life of the Virgin Mary. Look out for the pulpit decorated with the twelve apostles.

UNIVERSITY CHURCH★

Egyetemi templom
E6 – *Papnövelde utca 7* – Ⓜ *3, 4 Kálvin tér.*
The University Church of St Mary the Virgin is without doubt the most popular baroque church in the city. It was originally part of a monastery belonging to monks of the Order of

58

Saint Paul, the only religious order founded in Hungary, in the 13C and abolished in 1782. The exterior is impressive, with a pediment decorated with the order's insignia and flanked by two onion domes topped with crosses. The pediment also features statues of St Paul of Thebes and St Anthony. A carved wooden door leads to an interior decorated with frescoes (those on the dome depict scenes from the life of the Virgin Mary), marble-effect panelling, gilt ornamentation and carved wood. A copy of the Black Madonna of Częstochowa (in Poland) is in the choir above the altar. The **pulpit★★** was carved by the monks.

SERBIAN ORTHODOX CHURCH★

(Szerb templom)
E6 – Szerb utca 2–4 – Ⓜ *3, 4 Kálvin tér.*
This charming 18C church is a reminder that a community of Serbians was present in the district at one time. The church lies in an untended but tranquil garden behind high railings and thick ochre walls.

VÁCI UTCA★

(Váci Street)
D5–6 – Ⓜ *3, 4 Kálvin tér or* Ⓜ *3 Ferenciek tere.*
This is the one of the best **shopping streets** in Budapest, lined with stores of every description. Clothing, tableware, embroidery, confectionery, music, books, jewellery and much more besides. In high season this charming pedestrianised street also has more than its fair share of buskers and other street entertainers, all

seeking to divert passersby in the hope of a few forints' reward. You'll also find stalls selling postcards, guidebooks and illustrated books about the city. Tourists are also well catered for with cafés and bureaux de change.
When you need a break from the shops, it's worth glancing upwards to look at some of the building façades, such as no. 5, no.11a (Art Nouveau), no. 13 (neoclassical), no. 15 (carved wooden façade) and no. 18 (ceramic decoration). On the corner of Váci utca and Régiposta utca you will find the **Fountain of Hermes (Hermész-díszkút)**, the messenger of the gods and, appropriately enough, also the god of trade.
If you haven't quite managed to find what you want yet, there are plenty of other shopping streets in the area around Váci utca, including: **Petőfi Sándor utca**, **Párizsi utca**, **Haris köz**, and **Kígyó utca**.

PARIS COURT★

(Párisi udvar)
D6 – Entrance on Szabadsajtó út – Ⓜ *3 Ferenciek tere – closed for refurbishment until further notice.*
This lovely old shopping arcade contains a mix of architectural styles, with Byzantine, Moorish, Venetian, Renaissance and neo-Gothic elements all in evidence, not to mention the ubiquitous Art Nouveau. Its name is an allusion to the covered passages that were fashionable in Paris at the end of the 19C.

VÁROSHÁZ UTCA

(Városház Street)
D5–6 – Ⓜ *3 Ferenciek tere.*
Two municipal buildings occupy this street: **City Hall (Polgármesteri hivatal)** was designed by Austrian architect Anton Erhard Martinelli during the late baroque period (post 1710), although its appearance is more early baroque in style. Its proportions are simple, with rooms and halls connected by corridors beneath high vaulted ceilings. The building was originally a home for disabled soldiers. It is now the principal city hall in Budapest – each district has one. **Pest District Council (Pest megyei Önkormányzat)** has occupied a green neoclassical building here since 1895. As the plaques in the courtyard confirm, famous Hunarian politicians (Lajos Kossuth, István Széchenyi) and writers (Sándor Petőfi) all worked in the building in the past. There is no charge to enter the courtyard.

SZERVITA TÉR

(Szervita Square)
D5 – Ⓜ *3 Ferenciek tere.*
Two remarkable buildings look out onto this tiny square. The sleek modern lower half of the old **Török Bank** building (no. 3) belies its ornate upper half bearing a lovely allegorical mosaic of the History of Hungary. The **Rózsavölgyi House** (no. 5) is currently home to a record shop (with a concert space on the first floor). It features stylized motifs taken from traditional folklore that anticipate Art Deco (friezes separate the different floors). The building dates to 1912 and was designed by **Béla Lajta**, one of the forerunners of modern architecture in Hungary (♿ *p. 130*).

VÖRÖSMARTY TÉR★

(Vörösmarty Square)
D5 – Ⓜ *1 Vörösmarty tér.*
Every tourist visits this square at least once during their stay; its location in the heart of the pedestrianised district makes it unmissable. You will find a Carrara marble **monument to Mihály Vörösmarty** in the centre, a Romantic poet of the first half of the 19C (1800–1855) who was also a fervent patriot. The plinth features several characters declaiming lines from his well-known poem *Szózat* (*Exhortation*, 1840), which once it had been put to music became a patriotic song and almost a second national anthem. Often heard at ceremonial reunions, it ends:
Remain loyal to your country Hungarians, it is your cradle.
It has nourished you from its flesh And it will be your tomb.

Sándor Petőfi (1823–1849)
This poet played a key role on 15 March 1848, during the revolution of that year, spurring on the citizens of Pest with his poem 'National Anthem', a call to arms to fight for the freedom of Hungary. He has gone down in history as a key figure of the 1848 Revolution. He is believed to have died at the Battle of Segesvár, but his body was never found.

In summer, the monument is surrounded by buskers, painters, portrait artists and caricaturists. The crowds spill out onto the café terraces and this is where you will find the famous **Café Gerbeaud★**, a meeting-place for the socialites of the early 20C. The interior is totally 'turn-of-the-century' – very ornate with elaborate drapes, wood panelling, candlesticks and chandeliers, and the cakes are pretty special too, including some made to traditional Hungarian recipes (**⟲** *p. 92*). The building occupying the corner plot with Deák Ferenc utca dates from 1911. It once housed a large clothing store.

PESTI VIGADÓ ★

(Vigadó Palace building)
D5 – Ⓜ *1 Vörösmarty tér.*
The palace building is a very fine example of the style known as Hungarian Romanticism. It was constructed between 1859 and 1864 to designs by Frigyes Feszl to provide a venue for important ceremonies, concerts, balls and other spectacles. It remains one of the most famous concert hall venues in the city. The tall façade of the side giving onto the square is punctuated with columns topped with crowns and lavishly decorated with sculptures, making for a fairly busy overall impression.

DANUBE PROMENADE★★

(Duna korzó)
D5–6 – Ⓜ *3 Ferenciek tere.*
This promenade, which runs along the river from Széchenyi tér to Petőfi tér (look out for the statue of the poet Sándor Petőfi in front of the Marriott Hotel), offers beautiful panoramic views of Budapest taking in the Danube, the Széchenyi Chain Bridge, the Elisabeth Bridge, Buda Castle and Gellért Hill. The view is even more spectacular at night when everything is lit up.

INNER CITY PARISH CHURCH★

(Belvárosi plébánia templom)
D6 – Ⓜ *3 Ferenciek tere.*
The Inner–city Mother Church of the Blessed Virgin is the main parish church of Budapest and the oldest church in the Hungarian capital. It was built on the foundations of a Roman fort and is supposedly also the orginal burial place of St Gellért. With its two symmetrical bell towers rising either side of a porch topped with a pediment, it has become one of the symbols of the city. The building combines several styles, indicative of the different periods of its construction – the external Gothic buttresses contrast with the baroque façade, for example. Once through the porch, your gaze turns naturally to the vaulted Gothic choir with its mini spires, before which stands a triumphal arch. The baroque nave features a barrel vault and you will notice red marble tabernacles on the walls separating the choir from the nave. The church was converted into a mosque during the Turkish occupation, as can be seen from the mihrab in the apse, an ornamental niche marking the direction of Mecca for prayer, to the right of the choir.

Erzsébetváros★

(Jewish Quarter)

Bounded in broad terms by Károly körút, Erzsébet körút,
Dohány utca and Király utca, the old Jewish district is particularly suited to
exploring on foot. The area has also become a popular hangout for the young,
who dance the night away in the delapidated surroundings of its 'ruin bars',
which are busily reinventing the city's nightlife.

▶**Access:** Ⓜ 2 Astoria, Ⓜ 1 Deák Ferenc Tér; 🚊 47, 48, 49 Astoria; 🚌 7, 9 Astoria.
Detachable map EF 5.
▶**Tip:** Round off your visit to the Jewish Quarter with a visit to the Holocaust
Memorial Center in the Ferencváros district (♿ *p. 66*).
♿ *Addresses p. 87, 93, 97, 102 and 109.*

62

DOHÁNY STREET SYNAGOGUE★★

(Dohány utcai zsinagóga)
E5 *– Dohány utca 2 – Ⓜ 2 Astoria –*
trolley bus 74 Nagy Diófa utca –
℘ (1) 413 5584 – Mar–Apr & Oct
Sun–Thur 10am–6pm (Fri 4pm),
May–Sept Sun–Thur 10am–8pm
(Fri 4 pm), Nov–Feb Sun–Thur

10am–4pm (Fri 2pm), – closed Sat &
Jewish holidays – Ft4,000 (reduced
price with the Budapest Card).
With a capacity of 3,000, it is the
largest synagogue in Europe (and the
second-largest in the world after the
Temple Emanu-El in New York). Built
between 1854 and 1859 to a design
by the Viennese architect Ludwig

The Jewish community in Budapest

Having arrived mainly from Central Europe in the 17–18C, the Jews first settled in Buda
in the area around the castle. The early years were difficult for the new community until
Emperor Joseph II signed an Edict of Tolerance (1783) which accorded them the same
rights as Christians. The Jews settled in Pest during the second half of the 19C in the wake
of a law permitting them to own land. By the end of that century, the Jewish community,
now 170,000 strong, was one of the most closely integrated in Europe. A wave of anti-
Semitism arose after the First World War and, having allied itself with Nazi Germany,
Hungary promoted anti-Jewish legislation from 1938 onwards. The situation worsened in
the spring of 1944, when Germany occupied Hungary. By the end of 1944, the Jews in the
capital had been confined to a ghetto, while those elsewhere in Hungary were murdered
or deported by the Arrow Cross Party, the fascist faction that came to power in October of
that year. It has been estimated that 90 per cent of Hungary's 600,000 Jews died during
the Second World War.

Förster and taking its inspiration from Byzantine and Moorish architecture, it is a very beautiful brick building decorated with ceramic tiles and topped with two onion domes that resemble minarets. Inside there are two levels, around which run wooden galleries, while two great chandeliers hang over the central aisle (each weighing 1.5 tonnes). The interior is magnificent; note the rich decoration, especially the vaulted ceiling and the Ark of the Covenant, where the sacred Torah is kept, the roll of parchment bearing the Law of Moses.

Jewish Museum
(Magyar Zsidó Múzeum)
The history and traditions of the Hungarian Jews are illustrated with a variety of objects, manuscripts, textiles and information panels.

Raoul Wallenberg Holocaust Memorial Park
(Raoul Wallenberg Emlékpark)
Some 2,000 people lie buried in this garden, where a weeping willow, sculpted in steel (1991) by **Imre Varga**, honours the memory of the Hungarian Jews murdered during the Second World War. A plaque has been dedicated to the Righteous Among the Nations, including **Raoul Wallenberg**, the Swedish diplomat who risked his life to provide safe conduct for tens of thousands of Jews. After the liberation of Budapest, the Red Army sent him to the USSR, where he disappeared; his execution by the Soviet authorities was acknowledged only in 2000.

CARL LUTZ MEMORIAL
(Lutz Carl emlékmű)
E5 At **no. 12 Dob utca**, you will find a monument depicting a man lying on his back, attempting to get up and asking for help from an angel; it is a tribute to Carl Lutz (1895–1975), a Swiss diplomat who helped over 62,000 Jews find safety during the German occupation in the 1940s, even though his own life was in danger.

RUMBACH STREET SYNAGOGUE★
(Rumbach zsinagóga)
E5 – *Rumbach Sebestyén utca 11–13* – Ⓜ *2 Astoria* – *Closed for works, date for reopening not yet confirmed.*
This early work by the Viennese architect Otto Wagner was built between 1869 and 1872. The building's façade, with its multicoloured bricks and two towers that resemble minarets (a feature shared with the Dohány Street Synagogue), has a Moorish flavor – as has the interior, with its octagonal floorplan and rich ornamentation.

NEW YORK CAFÉ★
(New York Kávéház)
F5 – *Erzébet krt. 9–11* – Ⓜ *2 Blaha L. tér* – ♿ *p. 93.*
The New York Palace was built for an American insurance company between 1891 and 1895. By the turn of the 20C, the café had become very popular among journalists, writers and poets. The building has been restored and now houses a luxury hotel, of which the café is now part.

Kerepesi Cemetery and Ferencváros

If you are interested in architecture, and Secessionist-style art in particular, you won't want to leave Budapest without visiting the Museum of Applied Arts. And if you have time to explore the surrounding area further try the Kerepesi Cemetery before joining the relaxed pace of life in Ferencváros. This is an old (19C) working-class quarter that has become a bastion of middle-class Bohemianism, popular with families for its proximity to the Danube, its public parks and the Central Market Hall between its bustling boulevards. Finally, the slightly eccentric Ludwig Museum of Contemporary Art has a wealth of modern exhibits representing all aspects of the Hungarian avant-garde.

▶**Access:** For Kerepesi Cemetery: Ⓜ 2 or 4 Keleti pályaudvar; 🚊 24 Dologház utca. For Ferencváros: Ⓜ 3 Corvin-negyed; 🚊 4, 6 Corvin-negyed.
Detachable map GH 5–8 and EF 7–8.
▶**Tip:** The surroundings of the central market hall make up for the prices, which are a little higher than elsewhere. But for those short on time, it's a good place to shop for souvenirs.
♿ *Addresses p. 88 and 98.*

KEREPESI CEMETERY★

(Kerepesi Temető)

GH 5–6 – Fiumei út 16 – Ⓜ *2, 4 Keleti pályaudvar* – *Nov–Feb 7.30am–5pm, Mar 7am–5.30pm, Apr & Oct 7am–7pm, May–Jul 7am–8pm, Sept 7am–6pm, Oct 7am–5pm* – *free entry.* This landscaped cemetery, similar to London's Highgate Cemetery, was opened in 1847. Its grand, tree-lined avenues offer encounters with the bourgeoisie of the Austro-Hungarian Empire, bigwigs from the Communist occupation and a pantheon from among the working class. Some of the tombs are a pretext for a number of sculptoral fantasies (fabric carved in stone on the tomb of Antall József or the cherubs at the base of the sleeping effigy of Lujza Blaha, a famous Hungarian actress). Several celebrities are buried here, including poets Mihály Vörösmarty and Attila József, along with politicians Ferenc Deák, Lajos Batthyány and Lajos Kossuth. Thought to be the largest sculpture park in Europe, it is also popular with photographers in search of unusual subject matter. Near the main entrance is the small **Piety Museum** and **Collection of Funeral Culture**, illustrating Hungarian rituals associated with death and the accoutrements of funerals *(Mon–Fri 9am–5pm, Sat 10am-2pm – free).*

HOLOCAUST MEMORIAL CENTER★

(Holokauszt Emlékközpont)

F8 - *Páva utca 39* - Ⓜ *3 Corvin-negyed* - *℘ (1) 455 3333* - *hdke.hu* - *10am-6pm* - *closed Mon* - *Ft1,400 (reduced price with the Budapest Card)* - *audioguide in English Ft850. Not recommended for children.*

The Holocaust Memorial Center is both a museum and exhibition hall, as well as a research institute with a pedagogic mission. It presents a disturbing picture of the Holocaust in Hungary, depicting how victims (Jews and the Romanis) were stripped of their rights and exterminated, through the use of impactful modern media (recorded sound, film projections, interactive terminals, etc.).

66

PAUL STREET BOYS

F7 - *Práter utca 11-15* - Ⓜ *3 Corvin-negyed.*

This bronze sculpture depicts a game of marbles played by boys in a scene from the eponymous novel written by Ferenc Molnár (1878-1952), the popular Hungarian writer. It was installed in 2007 to mark the centenary of the work's publication.

MUSEUM OF APPLIED ARTS★★

(Iparművészeti Múzeum)

F7 - *Üllői út 33-37* - Ⓜ *3 Corvin-negyed* - *www.imm.hu* - *closed for refurbishment until end 2020.*

First opening its doors in 1896 on the occasion of Hungary's millennium celebrations, the building itself is one of the city's unmissable sights. The architect **Ödön Lechner** (statue in front of the museum), nicknamed the 'Hungarian Gaudí', was an ardent exponent of the Secession style, the Hungarian offshoot of Art Nouveau (♿ *p. 130*). You can judge for yourself how successful he was by standing outside the building and looking up at the façades and roofs where you'll find a profusion of colourful ornamentation, with ceramic tiles featuring floral and animal patterns. The ceiling in the entrance hall, is a riot of flowers. The interior is rather more subdued but still quite amazing; beneath a large metal-framed skylight, a vast hall is lined with dazzling white colonnades and balustrades. The museum's holdings include hundreds of items relating to European arts and crafts, arranged under broad themes: porcelain, ceramics, glassware; the art of the book, leather, bookbinding, paper; textiles; wood, joinery, cabinet-making; metal and ironwork.

☻ A selection of the museum's holdings is currently on display at the György Ráth Villa (♿ *p. 49*).

CENTRAL MARKET HALL★★

(Vásárcsarnok)

E7 - *Vámház krt. 1-3* - Ⓜ *4 Fővám tér* Ⓣ *2, 47, 48, 49* - *www.piaconline.hu* - *Mon 6am-5pm, Tue-Fri 6am-6pm, Sat 6am-3pm* ♿ *p. 98.*

In every city, at one time or another during their stay, most visitors make a beeline for the market, to wander around and soak up local life. But before embarking on some shopping, both the interior and the exterior of the Central Market Hall are worthy

Museum of Applied Arts

of attention. With its brick façade, neo-Gothic towers, roofs covered with Zsolnay majolica and the clock on its central section, from the outside the market hall could be mistaken for a railway station. Built at the end of the 19C, it was part of a project involving five covered markets designed by the architect Samu Petz. The city authorities chose to replace the original open-air markets with covered strutures, in order to contain any unpleasant odours, believed to be harmful to health.

On the ground floor, the cathedral-like interior beneath an iron frame houses a mass of colourful stalls heaving with fruit and vegetables, strings of garlic and garlands of peppers, not to mention immense salamis. It's worth doing a quick recce before you buy – you may find prices a little cheaper further away from the entrance. You will also find local alcoholic tipples, such as the famed apricot brandy (*barackpálinka*) and Unicum liqueur. The first floor consists of a gallery that runs around the market's perimeter where you will find bars, stalls selling snacks and Hungarian wines, craft objects, and, to round everything off, several stalls with a selection of embroidered table linens featuring infinite variations on motifs from Hungarian folklore.

BÁLNA ★

('The Whale')
E7-8 – Fővám tér 11-12 – Ⓜ *4 Fővám tér* – 🚊 *2 Zsil utca – www.balna budapest.hu – 10am-8pm (10pm Fri–Sat).*

A quick word about about the name of this **shopping and cultural centre**. It was nicknamed *bálna* or 'the whale' by the citizens of Budapest thanks to the building's shape; the name stuck and eventually it was officially renamed as such. While its futuristic silhouette radically changes the skyline here, it has nonetheless found its own place within the landscape, not least because it has been built on the shells of two old warehouses that have been now repurposed The 'belly' houses shops and some lovely restaurants, with a terrace looking out over the river, that are perfect for lunch or a sundowner, while the **New Budapest Gallery (Új Budapest Galéria)** has found a home on the first floor with an exhibition space dedicated to contemporary art.
📞 *(1) 388 6784 – budapestgaleria.hu – 10am–6pm – closed Mon – Ft1,000 (free with the Budapest Card).*

LUDWIG MUSEUM OF CONTEMPORARY ART★★

(Ludwig Múzeum Budapest)
Off map *– Komor Marcell utca 1 – HÉV 7 Közvágóhíd –* 🚊 *1, 2 Közvágóhíd –* 📞 *(1) 555 3444 – www.lumu.hu – Permanent collection 3rd floor 10am–6pm (temporary exhibitions 1st & 2nd floors, 8pm) – closed Mon – permanent collection Ft1,600 (free with the Budapest Card).*

The Ludwig Museum of Contemporary Art moved to the arts complex **MÜPA Budapest** in 2005 where it occupies one wing. If you fancy a change from the ubiquitous baroque

© Hungarian Tourism Agency

Ludwig Museum of Contemporary Art

and Scessionist styles, this is the place to come. It is Hungary's only museum dedicated exclusively to contemporary art. The exhibition space of more than 2,700sq m is spread over three floors. The first two are reserved for temporary exhibitions by Hungarian and international artists. The permanent collection, a gift from Irene and Peter Ludwig (a German chocolate manufacturer and a passionate collector – notably of Picasso – with 800 paintings, the largest collection in the world), is displayed on the third floor. The work of Hungarian artists is not neglected, while most works by Central and Eastern European artists date from the 1990s.

The permanent collection is not limited to the Ludwigs' donation as the museum continues to acquire works, some 20–30 a year, thanks to grants and the continued support of the Ludwig Foundation. Among the best-known names of the great movements in modern art are Pablo Picasso, Roy Lichtenstein, Jean Tinguely, Frank Stella, Joseph Beuys, Robert Rauschenberg, Claes Oldenburg, Andy Warhol and Jasper Johns. There is also a work by Yoko Ono – a white chessboard placed on a white table. The Hungarian avant-garde (1956–1958) has not been forgotten, nor a new generation of artists such as László Bartha, Béla Kondor, István Mazzag among others.

Margitsziget★★
(Margaret Island)

Margaret Island stretches out in a long almond shape (2.5 km long and 500m wide) between Margaret Bridge and Árpád Bridge, which both cross it, one at either end. A haven of peace and greenery, far from the noise of traffic (cars are banned here), it is particularly attractive in spring and is rightly considered one of the most beautiful parks in the capital.

▶**Access:** Via the south of the island 🚋 4, 6 Margitsziget/Margit híd; HÉV 5 Margit híd; Ⓜ 3 Nyugati pályaudvar. Via the north: 🚋 1 Népfürdő utca/Árpád híd. To get around the island itself: 🚌 26. ***Detachable map C1–2.***

MARGARET BRIDGE

(Margit híd)
C2 Lying at the southern tip of the island, the bridge consists of two spans that meet in the middle. It was designed by French engineer Ernest Goüin. The elaborate statues that decorate the massive supporting pillars are best seen by boat from the river. A replica of the Holy Crown (♿ *p. 39*) carved in stone and complete with the crooked cross is on top of the central pillar. From the middle of the bridge there is a good **view★** of the Danube, straddled by the next crossing downriver, the Chain Bridge, and to the right Buda Castle and Matthias Church, with Gellért Hill in the distance; to the left is Pest and the Parliament Building.

CENTENNIAL MEMORIAL

(Centenáriumi emlékmű)
C1 Not far from the fountain marking the most southerly end of the island is the Centennial Memorial, a sculpture in bronze that was unveiled in 1972 to mark the centenary of the union of Buda, Pest and Óbuda. Inside the monument is an eclectic collection

A haven of peace
With the exception of bus no. 26, which crosses the island, a small road train that tours its perimeter and a few electric buggies, vehicles are banned on Margaret Island; only cyclists are permitted. That makes cyling the perfect way to find your way around and you can hire bikes close to the roundabout a little way in from the southern access to the island. Hungarian families arrive en masse over summer weekends. With its sports fields, swimming pool, beach, rose garden, shady paths, lawns and picnic areas, hotels and restaurants, everything is in place for some serious recreation and relaxation. The island also has its own spa resort (Danubius Health Spa Resort) with accommodation.

> ### *From Hare Island to Margaret Island*
> *The Romans living in the nearby city of Aquincum (⟨ p. 75) came to Margaret Island to treat their aches and pains with the island's thermal waters. It later became a hunting ground for the kings of the Árpád dynasty who named it Hare Island. By the 12C monks were founding religious communities here, and in the 13C, after having suffered several defeats at the hands of the Mongol invaders, King Béla IV vowed that his daughter Margit (Margaret) would devote her life to God if the country were to be liberated. True to his word, he built a convent – the ruins of which are still visible – for Dominican nuns and handed over his daughter, who was then aged just nine. Occupation by the Turks brought with it destruction of the island's religious buildings and it remained uninhabited until the end of the 18C before becoming the property of Joseph, archduke of Austria and palatine of Hungary, who transformed it into a vast leisure park.*

of nationalist and industrial symbols, including a ship's rudder, a propeller and a gear wheel.

PALATINUS STRAND BATHS

(Palatinus strand)
North of C1.
The vast Palatinus Strand Baths complex (⟨ p. 106) lies on the banks of the Danube, opposite Buda. The facilities (10 pools altogether) include a 40m swimming pool, a wave pool, children's pools, a slide pool and a beach. It gets pretty crowded in summer.

ARTISTS' PROMENADE

(Művész sétány)
The promenade, shaded by trees and lined with the busts of Hungarian artists such as Franz Liszt, Ferenc Erkel and Mór Jókai, runs down the centre of Margaret Island and leads to a neo-Romanesque chapel. The scent of roses wafts through from the nearby **rose garden** in May and June.

DOMINICAN CONVENT

(Domonkos kolostor)
The ruins of this convent, to which Margaret, daughter of King Béla IV retired as a child, are visible among the greenery in the centre of the island (see panel above) .

OPEN-AIR THEATRE

(Szabadtéri színpad)
Located at the foot of the old **water tower** (1911, 57m high), you will find the large **open-air theatre** (⟨ p. 104), where dance spectaculars, concerts and opera are staged during the summer season.

MUSICAL FOUNTAIN

(Zenélő kút)
A great free attraction, in summer the fountain plays on the hour 10am–10pm, spraying water in time to the music (all genres) and is particularly magical at night when the fountain is floodlit against the trees.

Rózsadomb

(Rose Hill)

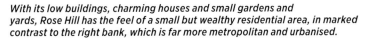

With its low buildings, charming houses and small gardens and yards, Rose Hill has the feel of a small but wealthy residential area, in marked contrast to the right bank, which is far more metropolitan and urbanised.

▶**Access:** Bus 91; 🚊 4, 6, 17; HÉV 5 Margit híd.
Detachable map BC 1–2.

GÜL BABA UTCA

(Gül Baba Street)

B1 This narrow street is admittedly charming and picturesque, but if you decide to start at the bottom and climb up, you'll find it very steep and the ground very uneven; best avoided in high heels.

TOMB OF GÜL BABA

(Gül Baba türbe)

B2 – Mecset utca 14 – 📞 (1) 237 4400. Halfway along Gül Baba utca are steps leading to the Tomb of Gül Baba, an octogonal structure with a domed roof and a crescent on top. This building, whose upkeep is the responsibility of the Turkish government, has become a place of pilgrimage for Muslims from all over the world. Gül Baba, known as the 'Father of Roses' because he is said to have introduced the rose to Hungary, was a dervish of the Bektashi Order (a statue at the entrance depicts him with a rose in his turban). He lived in the 16C and took part in the conquest of Buda, but much of what is known about him today is based on legend.

He is said to have died during a religious ceremony held in Matthias Church, which had been transformed into a mosque for the ooccasion. The sultan, Süleyman the Magnificent, attended his funeral in person and is said to have helped carry the coffin. Inside, the tomb itself is covered with a green cloth featuring verses from the Quran. Prayer mats and religious objects are also to be found within the tomb.

LUKÁCS BATHS★

(Lukács Gyógyfürdő)

C1 – Frankel Leó út 25–29 – ♿ p. 106. The baths are medieval (12C) in origin but were rebuilt in 1884 and renovated in 2012. Compared with other baths in Budapest, the design is fairly plain and the decoration is rather low key, but there are indoor and outdoor pools at temperatures between 22°C and 40°C, a Kneipp (wading) pool, saunas and a sundeck. Some people come here for the leafy garden area, which has become a meeting place for artists and is a welcome retreat from the heat in summer.

Óbuda and the Buda Hills★

Óbuda is the third of the city's twenty-three districts and was a separate town until 1873. It is the oldest part of Budapest – the Romans established the principal town of the Roman province Pannonia here. They created both a garrison town and, nearby, a municipium, a 'civilian municipality' named Aquincum, significant traces of which still remain and can be visited. Not far away, the Buda Hills provide an opportunity to get out of the city into the countryside, all the more enjoyable as they are so close and you don't have to travel far to breathe in some fresh air and enjoy great views over the capital.

▶**Access:** North of Buda – HÉV 5 towards Szentendre.
Off the detachable map.

ÓBUDA★

Fő tér★
HÉV 5 Szentlélek tér.
This small **cobbled square** surrounded by affluent, baroque-style buildings, has a distinct provincial feel. The surrounding streets are lined with brightly painted houses and old-fashioned lampposts, and in summer the terraces of the cafés and restaurants are full of passersby who have been tempted into stopping for a snack or a drink. This pleasant, tranquil area belies the fact that nearby are some of the impersonal buildings that flourished in Budapest thanks to the extensive urbanisation programme that was put in place in the 1960s. At the corner of Hajógyár utca and Laktanya utca you might be surprised to bump into **four women**, each sheltering beneath an umbrella. The group was cast in bronze by the contemporary artist and sculptor **Imre Varga** (born 1923), who has a number of other works dotted about the city, inlcuding the Holocaust Memorial.

Vasarely Museum★
(Vasarely Múzeum, Budapest)
Szentlélek tér 6 – HÉV 5 Szentlélek tér; 🚊 *1 – ☏ (1) 388 7551 – www.vasarely. hu – Daily except Mon 10am–5.45pm – Ft800 (free with the Budapest Card) – guided tours in English, but you must book at least 2 weeks in advance, Ft10,000 for a group of up to 15 persons.*
One of the leaders of the Op art movement, the artist **Victor Vasarely** (1908–1997) has donated to his home country several hundred of his works. They are now on display in the museum dedicated to him (renovated in 2017), housed in part of Zichy Castle. The pieces on display (paintings, drawings, tapestries) show

the evolution of his art, which makes use of optical illusions that combine geometric forms and colours to produce abstract images. Temporary exhibitions are also held here.

Hungarian Museum of Trade and Tourism
(Magyar kereskedelmi és vendéglátóipari Múzeum)
Korona tér 1 – HÉV 5 Szentlélek tér; Tram 1 – ℘ (1) 375 6249 – mkvm.hu – Daily except Mon 10am-6pm – Ft800 (free with the Budapest Card).
The house that once belonged to Hungarian writer Gyula Krúdy is now home to various advertising posters, crockery and other vintage objects connected to the world of trade. The reconstructions of old shops (selling hardware, confectionery and coffee, etc.) are likely to amuse the children.

Aquincum★
Szentendrei út 139 – HÉV 5 Aquincum then 15min walk or bus 134 Záhony utca; bus 34,106 Záhony utca – ℘ (1) 430 1081 – www.aquincum.hu – Museum Apr-Oct 10am-6pm, Nov-Mar 10am-4pm – ruins Apr-Oct 9am-6pm, rest of year depends on weather conditions – closed Mon – Ft1,600 (free with the Budapest Card).
The site comprises an archaeological park with the **ruins** of Aquincum (a site about 600 x 400m enclosed by protective walls) and an archeological **museum**. Aquincum was founded in the 1C and flourished in the 2C and 3C. Populated principally by tradesmen and craftsmen, it was once a very busy and active place, with Óbuda and Aquincum together comprising more than 60,000 inhabitants. Aquincum became a city in 124 CE under Emperor Hadrian, which meant it was governed according to its own laws while remaining under the authority of Rome. In 194 CE, under Emperor Septimus Severus, the city became a Roman colony, but at the end of the 4C it was subjected to attack by invaders from the east and went into decline, with the Huns administering the final blow in the 5C. The Romans abandoned Aquincum, but not before making a treaty with Attila, the new authority in the region.

Today, the layout of the city, with the outlines of streets and buildings, is clearly visible. The streets cross at right angles on a grid system above a network of sewers and water channels that lie amid the foundations of the various buildings. The public baths and the great covered market (*macellum*) stood opposite the museum, and beyond these were craftsmen's workshops, merchants' stalls and houses. At the far end of of the site a floor mosaic depicting wrestlers was uncovered in a small bathhouse that was part of a private home. A little further to the left is another small building (with a sundial beside the entrance) that contains more mosaics. Retracing your steps towards the museum, you will see a shrine to Mithras, the Persian god of the sun, who was worshipped by both the Greeks and the Romans, as well as the Painter's House, a reconstruction of a 3C home. Two buildings house exhibitions; the first, close to the entrance, explores the history of Budapest since the

74

Zuglieti chairlift

Paleolithic era, exhibiting finds from excavations carried out on the site (statues, bas-reliefs, coins, pottery, tools and everyday objects), along with temporary exhibitions. Children will enjoy the virtual games – take on a gladiator if you dare! The second building, the furthest away, also houses temporary exhibitions.

BUDA HILLS

(Budai–Hegység)

This lovely green landscape lies to the west of Buda, just a few miles from the noisy city, which can be stifling on hot days. There are trails to walk or cycle, picnic areas and panoramic viewpoints. In winter, with enough snow, the scene changes to one of winter sports with cross-country skiing, some downhill skiing and sledging.

Children's Railway★
(Gyermekvasút)

Széchenyi-hegy and Hűvösvölgy – Tram 56, 56A, 59B, 61 to Hűvösvölgy, get off at Városmajor, then take the Cog Railway (service 60) to Széchenyi-hegy – ℘ (1) 397 5394 – www.gyermekvasut.hu – Usually 9am–6pm (times vary according to season) – closed Mon (except in summer) – Ft1,400 round trip, children Ft700.

The Children's Railway or **Pioneer's Railway** (built in 1951 and named for the youth movement under the old regime) is a charming attraction. The nicest and most appropriate way to get there is to take the small Cog Railway (also designated tram 60) from outside the Hotel Budapest,

easily recognizable thanks to its circular shape *(Szilágyi Erzsébet fasor 47, not far from the park Városmajor)*, to Széchenyi-hegy terminus. From here head towards the television tower, near which you will find the small Children's Railway station. Apart from the engine, which is operated by an adult, the whole railway is staffed by children dressed in regulation uniforms, who salute each departure and arrival in a military fashion. The mostly wooded 12km route is charming, punctuated with several station stops, at any of which you can get off to take a walk in the surrounding woodland.

One way back to the city is via the fourth stop, János-hegy, from where you take the chairlift *(700m to the east, see below)* to Zugligeti út, then bus 291 to Nyugati Station via Margaret Bridge. Or bus 158 or tram 56 from Széchenyi-hegy to Széll Kálmán tér.

János–hegy (János Hill)

Bus 291 to Nyugati pályaudvar, Zugliget terminus, then the chairlift **Libegő** *– ℘ (1) 391 0352 – bkk.hu – Times of operation vary according to daylight hours (high season: 9am–7pm) – Ft1400 round trip.* János-hegy is the highest point in Buda (526m). At the top, take the road to the right that leads to a neo-Romanesque observation tower from where there is a magnificent **panoramic view★★**.

⊙ You can also reach the tower via the Children's Railway. Get off at János-hegy station then take the path that leads into the woods (around a 30min walk).

South of Budapest

While they are geographically close, Memento Park and Nagytétényi Palace Museum are otherwise worlds apart; the park is a fascinating relic from the Communist era, while the palace exhibits antique furniture. They are both worth a detour, not least as they can be reached easily and quickly on public transport.

OPEN-AIR MUSEUM★

(Memento Park)

15km south of the city centre – Ⓜ 4 Kelenföld pályaudvar, then bus 101 or 150 to Memento Park (15–30min journey); direct bus from Ⓜ Deák tér at 11am (look for the hostess on the pavement opposite the Ritz-Carlton Hotel, Ft4,900, including entrance) – ✆ (1) 424 7500 – www.mementopark. hu – 10am–sunset – Ft1,500 (reduced price with the Budapest Card) – guided tour in English daily at 11.45am (Ft1,200 per person).

If you have little experience of Communist era propaganda, Memento Park will prove quite an eye-opener. Monumental statues and groups of figures erected during the Communist regime have been reassembled in this park specially created for the purpose. They were dedicated to the glory of various of the era's significant figures and causes, from workers' movements and Soviet-Hungarian friendship to the Hungarian Brigade that fought in the Spanish Civil War, and so on. The whole effect is distinctly .... monumental. Opposite the entrance, a gigantic replica of a pair of Stalin's boots give an idea of the size of the original statue; it once stood behind

the Hall of Art (👁 p. 54) and was torn down by protesters during the 1956 Revolution. The cinema (opposite the entrance) shows films about the secret service and their pernicious procedures. The museum shop sells Soviet passports and posters, magnets and mugs adorned with Communist symbols.

NAGYTÉTÉNYI PALACE MUSEUM★

(Nagytétényi Kastélymúzeum)

15km southwest of the city centre – Kastélypark utca 9 – Ⓜ 4 Móricz Zsigmond körtér, then bus no. 33 or 33A to Petőfi Sándor utca and 5min walk – ✆ (1) 207 0005 – www.imm.hu – closed for refurbishment; date for reopening not yet confirmed.

Originally constructed in the 18C, the building's original contents were destroyed in a fire in 1904. The building suffered further damage in the Second World War, after which it was decided to put it to use holding exhibitions. The palace now houses an interesting collection of antique furniture (from the Museum of Applied Arts), with pieces that demonstrate the skill of craftsmen from the Middle Ages to the 19C.

Royal Palace of Gödöllő★★

(Gödöllői Királyi Kastély)

The town of Gödöllő (pronounced Geur-deur-leur) attracts locals and tourists alike to its royal palace, a place soaked in history and linked to the memory of the Emperor Franz Joseph and the Empress Elisabeth, better known as Sisi.

▶**Access:** 28km northeast of Budapest. Ⓜ 2 to Örs vezér tere, then HÉV 8 to Gödöllő Szabadság tér.

℘ 28 410 124 – www.kiralyikastely.hu – Apr–Oct 10am–6pm, Nov–Mar 10am–4pm (weekends & Christmas holidays 5pm) – Ft2,600 – guided tour for up to 9 people Ft6,500 – audioguide in English Ft800.

Believed to be the largest Hungarian baroque castle, the palace itself covers nearly half an acre (1,700sq m) and the park 69 acres (28 ha). Set into the main façade is a large porch topped with a dome and fronted with a beautiful wrought-iron balcony supported by four sets of twin columns in red marble and decorated with Ionic capitals. The coat of arms in the centre of the balustrade belongs to the aristocratic Grassalkovich family. Unusually, there are seven wings, which fan out from the rear of the building. The royal apartments have been faithfully reconstructed and there is an exhibition paying tribute to the well-known beauty Empress Sisi. One section is devoted to the Grassalkovich era, focussing on the castle's baroque history. You can also see a baroque theatre *(visit by guided tour only, weekends, Ft1,200 per person).*

A mixed history

Count Antal Grassalkovich I began construction of the palace in the 18C. In 1867, after the Grassalkovich family line died out, the Hungarian state took over possession and after renovation work directed by architect Miklós Ybl, the palace was offered to Emperor Franz Joseph and his consort Elisabeth for their coronation as sovereigns of Hungary that same year. The royal family enjoyed their visits to Gödöllő, finally able to relax far from the stuffy protocol of the court at Vienna. In 1920, directly after becoming Regent, Hungarian statesman Miklós Horthy made the palace his official residence and had an air raid shelter constructed in the garden. German troops sacked the palace during the Second World War and Soviet troops turned it into a military hospital. It fell into decay after the war until its rehabilitation finally began in 1981.

Addresses

81

You can also find the addresses
in The Michelin Guide: Main
Cities of Europe by scanning
the image opposite

Rooftop bar, Hotel President Budapest,
with a view to the parliament and Postal Savings Bank
© Hungarian Tourism Agency

🍴
Where to eat

There are many simple but very pleasant restaurants in the **Belváros** district, on Ráday utca (Ⓜ 3 or 4 Kálvin tér). Or if you are in the mood to linger over your food until late in the evening, try the oblong-shaped 'square' Liszt Ferenc tér (Ⓜ 1 Oktogon), near **Andràssy út**. In the **Erzsébetváros** district, restaurants on Dob utca (Ⓜ 1, 2 or 3 Deák Ferenc tér) are a good bet. At lunchtime, most restaurants offer good value set menus *(mai menü)* as well as à la carte selections. The price ranges in this section correspond with the restaurants' fixed price menus or starter–main–dessert menus.

👌 *Types of eatery, p. 120; Hungarian cuisine, p. 135.*

👌 *Find the addresses on our maps using the number in the listing (for example ❶). The coordinates in red (for example C2) refer to the detachable map (inside the cover).*

BUDA CASTLE

Area map p. 16

Under Ft4,860
㉑ Zona – *C5* – Lánchíd utca 7/9 – 🚊 19, 41 – 📞 (30) 422 5981 – www.zonabudapest.com – 10am-midnight. An ideal spot for a coffee before or after the climb up to the castle, or for a tasty lunch attractively presented, such as salmon tartare or pork medallion with sweet potato purée. Jazz music on the first Wednesday evening in the month.

VÁRNEGYED

Area map p. 21

Ft4,860–9,720
❸ Café Pierrot – *B4* – Fortuna utca 14 – Ⓜ 2 Széll Kálmán tér – 📞 (1) 375 6971 – www.pierrot.hu – Midday–midnight. Traditional cooking and fine dining in elegant surroundings,with a subtle nod to Pierrot in the decor. A pleasant garden in which to eat in fine weather.
❹ 21 – *B4* – Fortuna utca 21 – Ⓜ 4 Széll Kálmán tér – 📞 (1) 202 2113 – 21restaurant.hu – Midday–midnight. Eat on the terrace during the day and inside, in the evening, in a friendly bistro-style ambience. The chef fuses traditional Hungarian cuisine with more contemporary flavours.

From Ft9,720
❺ Alabárdos – *B4* – Országház utca 2 – Ⓜ 4 Széll Kálmán tér – 📞 (1) 356 0851 – www.alabardos.hu – Daily except Sun, 7pm–11pm, Sat midday–3pm, 7pm–11pm. Overlooking the castle grounds, in a 17C building. Generous portions of the great traditional Hungarian dishes.

GELLÉRTHEGY

Under Ft4,860
😊 ❻ Pagony Kert – *D8* – Kemenes utca 10 – Ⓜ 4 Szent Gellért tér – 📞 (31) 783 6411 – www.pagonykert.hu – 📶 – Mon-Fri 9am-10pm, weekends

Onyx

11am–10pm. In a small street next to the Gellért Baths, this lovely outdoor café is open in summer in the gardens (*kert*) of a former pool complex. Some tables are even set up in the now empty small pools. Fresh, simple and tasty cooking. A delicious house lemonade. A great venue when the weather is fine.

1 Hummusbar – *D8* – *Bartók Béla út 6 – M 4 Szent Gellért tér – ℘ (1) 787 8888 – hummusbar.hu – Mon–Fri 10am–10pm, weekends midday–10pm.* One of a chain of restaurants offering Middle Eastern food (there are over a dozen in Budapest). On the menu: pitas, *shakshuka* (an egg-based dish), falafels and ... hummus, of course. Cheap and delicious. A healthy and tasty concept.

84

VÍZIVÁROS

Under Ft4,860

7 Nagyi Palacsintázója – *C3* – *Batthyány tér 5 – M 2 Batthyány tér – www.nagyipali.hu – 24hr.* One of a chain of crêperies with four locations in Budapest, this place is perfect for lunch on the go and is very popular with the locals. Food is served all day: *sós rakott tejföllel* (lasagne with a crêpe base and sour cream), or sweet crêpes with poppy seeds (*makos*), morello cherries (*meggyes*) or apple (*almas*)... Take your food up to the mezzanine level from where you can gaze out at the bustling square Batthyány tér and, beyond that, the Danube.

Ft4,860–9,720

8 Csalogány 26 – *B3* – *Csalogány utca 26 – M 2 Batthyány tér – ℘ (1) 201 7892 – www.csalogany26.hu – Daily except Sun & Mon, Tue–Thur midday–3pm, Fri–Sat midday–3pm, 7pm–10pm. Closed public holidays.* On the way down the hill from the castle, stop off in this restaurant to recharge your batteries. The decor is modern and the menu is seasonal and offers good value.

LIPÓTVÁROS

Under Ft4,860

9 Nemsüti – *D2* – *Jászai Mari tér 4/b – M 3 Nyugati pályaudvar, Tram 4, 6 Jászai Mari tér – ℘ (70) 621 1123 – nemsuti.hu – Mon–Fri 11am–5pm. Closed weekends.* Before heading off to explore Margaret Island, stop at this sandwich bar close to Margaret Bridge which is said to serve the best vegetarian meals in Budapest: salads and soups, along with more substantial dishes, delicious cakes and fruit juices.

From Ft9,720

11 Tom–George Italiano – *D4* – *Október 6 utca 8 – M 1 Bajcsy-Zslinszka. út – ℘ (20) 266 3525 – tomgeorge.hu – Midday–midnight.* A restaurant with a contemporary feel near the basilica in a street named for the day on which 13 generals were executed in the 1848 Revolution. Fusion food ('Italian style with a twist') and a stylish interior. Fresh, creative dishes with an eye on the Mediterranean as well as Hungary.

12 Borkonyha – *D5* – Sas utca 3 – Ⓜ *1 Bajcsy-Zslinszka. út* – ☎ *(1) 266 0835* – *www.borkonyha.hu* – *Daily except Sun and public holidays, midday–midnight, kitchen closed 4pm–6pm.* This elegant, airy and modern bistro close to the basilica marries Hungarian wines (over 200 to choose from, many served by the glass) with a refined cuisine using local products: pork cheeks, cabbage with saffron, duck liver with cinnamon or trout from northern Hungary.

ANDRÁSSY ÚT

Under Ft4,860

13 M Étterem – *E4* – Kertész utca 48 – Ⓜ *1 Opera or Oktogon,* 🚊 *4, 6 Király utca* – ☎ *(1) 322 3108* – *metterem.hu* – *Daily except Mon 6pm–midnight.* A stone's throw from the Music Academy, serving Hungarian cooking at reasonable prices. Frequented by arty types and the cosmopolitan friends of the owner.

14 Két Szerecsen – *E4* – Nagymező utca 14 – Ⓜ *1 Opera* – ☎ *(1) 343 1984* – *ketszerecsen.hu* – 📶 – *8am–midnight, weekends 9am–midnight.* This local bistro has a central location, a pleasant atmosphere and a clientele of regulars. It doesn't go so far as to offer fine dining but its soups, salads and Hungarian meals with a French twist hit the spot very nicely. You can eat on the terrace in summer.

15 Cech In – *E4* – Lázár utca 7 – Ⓜ *1 Opera,* Ⓜ *3 Arany János utca* – ☎ *(20) 298 9929* – 📶 – *Daily except Sun 4pm–1am.* Specialising in Czech beer, this friendly bar near the opera serves hearty Central European-style food at good prices, eaten at the counter or in the wood-panelled dining room.

Ft4,860–9,720

16 Menza – *E4* – Liszt Ferenc tér 2 – Ⓜ *1 Oktogon,* 🚊 *4, 6 Oktogon* – ☎ *(1) 413 1482* – *www.menza.co.hu* – *10am–midnight.* It's hard to miss this place on the popular Liszt Ferenc tér. Good Hungarian dishes are served in the midst of a 1950s socialist-style cantine decor. Usually packed and therefore noisy, but no complaints about the food and service.

17 Rickshaw – *F4* – Erzsébet körút 43–49 – Ⓜ *1 Oktogon,* 🚊 *4, 6 Király utca* – ☎ *(1) 479 4855* – *www.rickshaw.hu* – *Daily except Mon & Tue, 6pm–11pm.* Rickshaw has a reputation for serving the best Asian food in the city. People flock to this stylish restaurant belonging to the Corinthia Hotel to enjoy Thai, Malaysian and Chinese cooking, as well as excellent sushi from the Japanese chef. An elegant eastern Zen-style decor.

From Ft9,720

18 Klassz – *E4* – Andrássy út 41 – Ⓜ *1 Oktogon,* 🚊 *4, 6 Oktogon* – ☎ *(1) 599 9490* – *www.klasszetterem.hu* – *11.30am–11pm.* A chic spot, this restaurant wears its name well and doesn't let the equally classy Andrássy út down at all. A new and lighter take on the Hungarian gastronomic tradition and an interesting wine list. The staff are knowledgeable and the clientele fashionable. Booking is advised.

VÁROSLIGET

Ft4,860–9,720

20 Robinson – *G1* – Városligeti tó – 🗔 *1 Széchenyi Fürdő* – ✆ *(1) 422 0222* – *www.robinsonrestaurant.hu* – *Midday–11pm.* Situated right next to the water, on a wooded island in the lake in Városliget (City Park). Robinson offers the chance to escape the city noise and try Hungarian and Mediterranean cuisine while gazing across the lake to Vajdahunyad castle. A guitarist accompanies dinner in the evenings and there is a large terrace for summer dining that can accommodate 100 people, inside there is seating for a further 80. If meat is your thing, there is a steakhouse upstairs. If you'd like to know in whose illustrious celebrity footsteps you are following, David Bowie, Sylvester Stallone and Arnold Schwarzenegger have all dined here in the past.

BELVÁROS

Under Ft4,860

2 Oh my green – *D6* – Petőfi Sándor utca 10 – 🗔 *3 Ferenciek tere* – ✆ *(1) 321 0448* – *www.ohmygreen.hu* – *Mon–Fri 9am–7pm, Sat 10am–5pm. Closed Sun.* If the idea of Buddha bowls, chia seeds and Goji berries take your fancy, this is the place for you – a café with an attractive, warm, contemporary interior for an ultra healthy and well-presented snack full of flavour, as the name might suggest. Takeaway options are on offer too.

22 Károlyi Étterem & Kávéház – *E6* – Károlyi Mihály utca 16 – 🗔 *2 Astoria* – ✆ *(1) 328 0240* – *www.karolyietterem. hu* – *Midday–11pm.* In a lovely elegant and historic setting – the courtyard of the town house of the counts of Károly, shaded by huge trees. The menu is essentially Hungarian but includes the odd nod to European menus. It's worth asking re any food intolerances or allergies – gluten-free and vegan options are often also on offer. The wine list includes all the major Hungarian vintages and a pianist entertains after 7pm.

23 Fatâl – *D6* – Váci utca 67 – 🗔 *3, 4 Kálvin tér,* 🗔 *3 Ferenciek tere* – ✆ *(1) 266 2607* – *www.fatalrestaurant. com* – ⊟ – *Midday–midnight.* People are usually happy to queue to eat here on account of its unique atmosphere. Design-wise: a long cellar with a vaulted ceiling, communal tables, a jolly and rustic ambience. Food-wise: the generous and substantial dishes are served on wooden boards (*fatál*) or directly in the pots and pans that cooked them. Watch out for the vast portions!

Ft4,860–9,720

25 Kárpátia – *E6* – Ferenciek tere 7–8 – 🗔 *3 Ferenciek tere* – ✆ *(1) 317 3596* – *www.karpatia.hu* – *11am–11pm, Sat & Sun 5pm–11pm. Closed 24 Dec.* This classic central Budapest address on Ferenciek tere has been serving traditional Hungarian food since 1877 and now offers new Hungarian cuisine too. Crisp tablecloths and napkins await you in an ornate dining room with hand-painted decoration on the walls.

26 Múzeum – *E6* – *Múzeum körút 12 –* Ⓜ *2 Astoria –* ✆ *(1) 338 4221 – www.muzeumkavehaz.hu – Mon–Sat 6pm–midnight. Closed Sun and public holidays.* A good spot for lovers of traditional Hungarian cooking (pike-perch filet, trout, crêpes Hortobágy)... it has been open since 1885. You will be dining in grand belle époque surroundings with faience tiles, wood detail in the decor and high ceilings.

From Ft9,720

27 Onyx – *D5* – *Vörösmarty tér 7–8 – entrance on Harmincad utca –* Ⓜ *1 Vörösmarty tér –* ✆ *(30) 508 0622 – www.onyxrestaurant.hu – Thur–Sat midday–2.30pm, Tue–Sat 6.30pm –11pm. Closed Sun & Mon.* The restaurant attached to the very grand Café Gerbeaud. With its gloved waiters and baroque decor, this is the best address in Budapest. Contemporary Hungarian cuisine at its finest: foie gras with morello cherries, black pudding with beetroot and chicory, suckling pig with smoked tomatoes.... And the best vintage wines to accompany your meal. Reservation essential.

ERZSÉBETVÁROS

Under Ft4,860

10 Passage Gozsdu – *E5* – *Gozsdu Udvar –* Ⓜ *1, 2 or 3 Deák Ferenc tér.* Tapas, goulash, Thai-style sauté noodles and Italian pasta.... The restaurants and bars in the Passage Gozsdu are popular with young people ... and tourists. Pleasant terraces where the beer flows freely on fine days.

29 Spinoza – *E5* – *Dob utca 15 –* Ⓜ *1, 2 or 3 Deák Ferenc tér –* ✆ *(1) 413 7488 - www.spinozahaz.hu – 8am–midnight.* In the heart of the Jewish quarter, schnitzels and traditional Hungarian cuisine in a musical ambience (piano music from 7pm). A breakfast menu is available all day. Regular concerts in the small theatre at the rear.

31 Kazimir – *E5* – *Kazinczy utca 34 –* Ⓜ *1, 2 or 3 Deák Ferenc tér –* ✆ *(20) 354 5533 - bistro.kazimir.hu – 10am–4am.* Opposite the orthodox synagogue, Kazimir puts the emphasis on tradition. A warm welcome and often a jazz concert (free!) at 9pm.

30 Karaván – *E5* – *Kazinczy utca 18 –* Ⓜ *2 Astoria or Blaha Lujza tér – 11.30am–midnight.* Street food reaches Budapest. A small open-air venue with several vans serving food to take away or eat at one of the tables provided: burgers, salads, crêpes, pasta, hot dogs and cold meats, Indian vegetarian dishes, ice creams.... There's something for everyone and all tastes.

28 Mazel Tov – *E4* – *Akácfa utca 47 –* 🚃 *4, 6 Erzsébet körót –* ✆ *(70) 626 4280 - mazeltov.hu – Mon–Wed midday–1am, Thur–Sat 10am–2am, Sun 10am–1am.* Delicious Israeli street food (*shawarma* sandwich) or something more elaborate (lamb with grilled aubergine) served in a very pleasant atrium. There's a jazz group in the evening and brunch on Sundays. Reservation essential if you don't want to eat in the less appealing dining room next door.

🍴

32 Kőleves – **E5** – *Kazinczy utca 41* –
Ⓜ *1, 2 or 3 Deák Ferenc tér* – ☎ *(1) 322
1011* – *www.kolevesvendeglo.hu* –
*Mon–Fri 8am–midnight, weekends
9am–midnight.* The atmosphere here
is relaxed and cosmopolitan. On the
menu is a choice of Jewish-influenced
dishes – not unnaturally, given its
location in the Jewish quarter – but
adapted to contemporary tastes.
Vegetarians and those in search of
'light bites' will enjoy the salads,
soups and attractive meat-free dishes.

Ft4,860–9,720

30 Bock Bisztró – **F4** – *Erzsébet
krt 43–49* – *Corinthia Hotel* – Ⓜ *1
Oktogon,* Ⓣ *4 or 6 Király utca* –
☎ *(1) 321 0340* – *www.bockbisztro.hu*
– *Daily except public holidays,
midday–4pm, 6pm–midnight.*
An elegant restaurant with Art
Deco touches, the atmosphere is
nevertheless more in the vein of
a small bistro. Classic Hungarian
cuisine mixed with lighter dishes,
tapas, cheese and cold cuts. Attentive
service. Bock has sister restaurants in
Buda and at Lake Balaton, the large
lake in western Hungary that is a very
popular tourist destination.

KEREPESI

Under Ft4,860

33 Csiga Cafe – **F6** – *Vásár utca 2* –
Ⓜ *4 Rákóczi tér* – ☎ *(30) 613 2046* –
9am–midnight. This small café with
the snail logo (*csiga*) attracts a loyal
clientele for its cosy ambience, music
and excellent but reasonably priced
menus, rare enough in this district
that is heading upmarket.

Ft4,860–9,720

34 Rosenstein – **G5** – *Mosonyi
utca 3* – Ⓜ *2, 4 Keleti pályaudvar,*
Ⓣ *24, 6 Keleti pályaudvar* –
☎ *(1) 333 3492* – *rosenstein.hu* – *Daily
except Sun, midday–11pm.* Tucked
away in a small street, Rosenstein
serves Hungarian and modern Jewish
food (soups, foie gras, roasts, fish
from Lake Balaton, venison, goose).
A fine selection of wines is on offer,
including red wine from Villány,
a town in southern Hungary that
has become one of Hungary's top
wine-growing regions. Rosenstein's
menu in 5 languages comprises a
substantial 28 pages!

FERENCVÁROS

Under Ft4,860

35 Paris–Texas Kávéház – **E7** –
Ráday utca 22 – Ⓜ *3, 4 Kálvin tér*
– ☎ *(1) 218 0570* – *Midday–3am.*
This address is good for lunch at
reasonable prices. Vegetarian and
Italian dishes are served in a 1900s
retro bistro-style. In summer, you can
eat on the terrace on the street, which
is one of the liveliest in the city.

Ft4,860–9,720

36 Vörös Postakocsi Étterem – **E7** –
Ráday utca 15 – Ⓜ *3, 4 Kálvin tér* –
☎ *(1) 217 6756* – *www.vorospk.hu* –
11am–midnight. Another place to try in
this street already full of restaurants,
many of which serve dishes with an
international influence. However,
this place is notable for only serving
Hungarian food, including typical
meat dishes.

Mazel Tov

Where to drink

What better or more typical way to while away a few hours in Budapest than by taking tea or coffee and a deliciously rich cake in one of the many **cukrászda** (patisserie-tea salon). But if you prefer a beer or a cocktail try the Belváros district or around St Stephen's Basilica, while Liszt Ferenc tér (Ⓜ *1 Oktogon*), the streets Kiraly and Dob utca (Ⓜ *1, 2 or 3 Deák Ferenc tér*) and Ráday utca (Ⓜ *3, 4 Kálvin tér, 3 Corvin-negyed*) are lively both day and night.

Ġ Find the addresses on our maps using the number in the listing (for example ❶). The coordinates in red (for example C2) refer to the detachable map (inside the cover).

VÁRNEGYED

Area map p. 21

Tea room

❶ **Ruszwurm Cukrászda** – *B4* – *Szentháromság utca 7 – ℘ (1) 375 5284 – www.ruszwurm.hu – 10am–7pm.* With Biedermeier-style decor and rich cakes and strudels, this is one of the oldest tea rooms in Hungary. Sisi, aka Empress Elizabeth of Austria and Queen Consort of Hungary used to come here in the 19C. It is also one of the busiest tea salons; locals and tourists line up patiently for a table in the charming small dining room which has remained unchanged since 1827. Cake and old-school nostalgia, what's not to like?

GELLÉRTHEGY

Wine bar

⓲ **Palack Wine Bar** – *D8* – *Szent Gellért tér 3 – Ⓜ 4 Szent Gellért tér – ℘ (30) 997 1902 – www.palackborbar. hu – Midday–midnight (11pm Mon, 10pm Sun).* A great place to discover Hungarian wine (a wide selection) while nibbling on tapas (ham, salami, cheese) in a relaxed atmosphere. Palack also organises tasting evenings and holds jazz concerts here.

VÍZIVÁROS

Café

❸ **Angelika Kávéház** – *C3* – *Batthyány tér 7 – Ⓜ 2 Batthyány tér, ⓣ 19, 41 Batthyány tér – ℘ (1) 225 1653 – www.angelikacafe.hu – 9am–11pm (midnight in summer). Closed 24 Dec.* This café is situated next door to an 18C church and beside the River Danube. Angelika Kávéház has a terrace with a great view of the Parliament Building, perfect on sunny days, or you can sit in one of the attractive rooms inside where you can try one of the many cakes and pastries, including the house speciality Angelika torta, a sort of sponge cake with chocolate and vanilla. They also serve main meals here, but the cakes are probably the better option.

LIPÓTVÁROS

Tea room

4 Európa Kávéház – *D2* – *Szent István krt 7–9* – Ⓜ *3 Nyugati pályaudvar,* 🚋 *19, 41 Jászai Mari tér* – 🕿 *(1) 312 2362* – *www.europakavehaz. hu* – *8.30am–8pm.* One of the best tea rooms in Budapest, situated beside Margaret Bridge. To get a table, try the upper floor. Among the tasty patisseries look out for those made with marzipan and nuts – a house speciality – as well as the Sachertorte, a rich chocolate cake said to have been invented in Vienna, and Black Forest gateau.

Bar

6 Raqpart – *D5* – *Jane Haining Rkp.* – Ⓜ *1 Vörösmarty tér,* 🚋 *2 Eötvös tér* – 🕿 *(30) 959 5352* – *www.raqpart.hu* – *June–Sept midday–1am (3am Fri & Sat).* The Raqpart's rather spectacular location – right by the Chain Bridge on the banks of the Danube – makes this open-air bar (only open in summer) one of the best places for a drink while watching the sun set over the castle and river. Electro disco beats meet wooden tables and decking. Come here for lunch or dinner too.

ANDRÁSSY ÚT

Tea room

7 Művész Kávéház – *E4* – *Andrássy út 29* – Ⓜ *1 Opera* – 🕿 *(1) 343 3544* – *muveszkavehaz.hu* – *8am–9pm, Sun and public holidays 9am–9pm.* This café is certainly one of the most expensive in town, but you can't beat the location (on the Budapest equivalent of the Champs–Élysées). The decoration is deliciously retro (wood, marble, chandeliers) and the list of particularly yummy patisseries provides an ample excuse to stop here and let time go drifting by, just for a while.

Café

10 Mai Manó Kávézó – *E4* – *Nagymező utca 20* – Ⓜ *1 Oktogon* – 🕿 *(1) 269 5642* – *8am–1am.* A North African-style café near the house of the famous photographer Mai Manó (now a centre for photography with a gallery and bookshop). The walls of this café are painted in an appropriate 'mint–tea green', while crimson velour banquettes, carpets and a profusion of cushions complete the exotic and intimate look. Enjoy coffee and a croissant or a glass of wine and just watch people go by.

Bar

13 MÜSZI Közért – *F4* – *Izabella utca 29* – 🕿 *(1) 295 6935* – *www.muszi.org* – Ⓜ *1 Vörösmarty tér.* Students, artists, intellectuals and local families come to this multi-faceted venue that can't quite be pinned down. Exhibitions and art, free university and co-working space, it is a community-inspired venue for multicultural experiment. A full programme of workshops, conferences, concerts and other performances are listed on Müszi's website.

BELVÁROS

Tea rooms

12 **Café Gerbeaud** – *D5* – *Vörösmarty tér 7–8* – Ⓜ *1 Vörösmarty tér* – ☎ *(1) 429 9000* – *www.gerbeaud.hu* – *9am–9pm.* The most famous café in Budapest, bought from its founder Henrik Kugler in 1884 by renowned Swiss confectioner Émile Gerbeaud. Franz Liszt was a regular, as was Hungarian first minister Ferenc Deák and it is still an institution today. With its palatial exterior and grand chandeliers, it is hugely popular with tourists who come here from all over the world, even if the quality of the patisseries is a little uneven. Choose a cake at the counter and a waitress will bring it to the table. You can also buy boxes of dainty chocolates and candies, which make good gifts to take home.

2 **Fruccola** – *D5* – *Kristóf tér 3* – Ⓜ *1 Vörösmarty tér* – ☎ *(1) 430 6125* – *fruccola.hu* – *Mon–Fri 7.30am–9pm, Sat 8am–9pm, Sun 8am–7pm.* Unusually for Budapest, they serve excellent fresh fruit juices here in this branch of Fruccola, one of three in the city. Eco-friendly, with vegan and vegetarian options, everything is prepared freshly in the shop. Get your daily vitamin hit with a mix of pineapple, coriander, spinach, lemon and orange juice. Cakes, sandwiches and salads are also on offer and there is a good choice of 'grab and go' takeaway options.

ERZSÉBETVÁROS

Tea rooms

☺ ⓐ 14 **Fröhlich Kóser Cukrászda** – *E5* – *Dob utca 22* – Ⓜ *2 Astoria or Blaha Lujza tér* – ☎ *(1) 266 1733* – *www.frohlich.hu* – *Daily except Sat 9am–6pm, Fri 9am–2pm.* Known for its Jewish patisseries, and therefore extra busy during Jewish festivals, this small kosher bakery and Ashkenazi café serves one of the best *flódni* in town, an apple cake with nuts and poppy seeds. A welcoming family ambience and a perfect place for a light lunch or snack.

15 **New York Café** – *F5* – *Erzsébet krt 9–11* – Ⓜ *2 Blaha Lujza tér* 🚊 *4, 6 Wesselényi utca* – ☎ *(1) 886 6167* – *www.newyorkcafe.hu* – *9am–midnight.* Drop in here just for the pleasure of discovering this legendary café. It fell on hard times and at one time was a sports goods shop, but was restored to its original splendour in 2006. A brunch menu (buffet until 11am) that suits families (free for under 8s) served in the downstairs room. Otherwise, prices are a bit high with afternoon tea for two at Ft19,500.

Café

19 **Massolit** – *E5* – *Nagy Diófa utca 30* – Ⓜ *2 Astoria or Blaha Lujza tér* – ☎ *(1) 788 5292* – *www.facebook.com/MassolitBudapest* – *Mon–Fri 8.30am–7.30pm, weekend 10am–7.30pm.* An unpretentious café-bookshop that's ideal for a quick break. A good choice of books in English and a nice small garden area.

93

🛍

Shopping

Fashion & accessories, designer items, interior decoration.... The last few years have seen a proliferation of shops in Budapest along with large commercial centres such as Mammut (🕭 *p. 29*) and Bálna (🕭 *p. 68*).

If you enjoy browsing antiques, try **Falk Miksa utca** in Lipótváros, while you'll find stores belonging to many of the famous luxury brands in the Belváros district, notably in the well-known pedestrian street **Váci utca** and other streets nearby. There are many shops to choose from and among them are some real gems. The area around the castle (Várnegyed) is inevitably touristy but is still also worth a look. Finally, if you are on the hunt for something different to take home food-wise, you'll find Hungarian food products such as the famous cream-filled snack bar *túró rudi* in the commercial centres (🕭 *p. 136*).

🕭 *Opening hours, p. 116.*

🕭 *Find the addresses on our maps using the number in the listing (for example ❶). The coordinates in red (for example C2) refer to the detachable map (inside the cover).*

VÁRNEGYED

Area map p. 21

Folk arts and crafts
⓬ Mester Porta Galéria – *C4* – *Corvin tér 7* – Ⓜ *2 Batthyány tér* – ☏ *(20) 232 5614* – *Tue–Sat 10.30am–6pm.* A useful place if

you are in search of gifts with a difference: clothes, colourful painted eggs, ceramic ware, jewellery and accessories, folk music CDs and some traditional costumes.

LIPÓTVÁROS

Antiques
❹ Pintér – *D3* – *Falk Miksa utca 10* – Ⓜ *2 Kossuth Lajos tér,* 🚋 *2 Országház* – ☏ *(1) 311 3030* – *www.pinterantik.hu* – *Mon–Fri 10am–6pm, Sat 10am–2pm.* The vast showroom (1,800sq m) of this antiques emporium occupying a series of cellars near the Parliament Building is crammed with furniture, paintings and all kinds of curious objects, some of which date back to the Renaissance. Many pieces are Hungarian, especially furniture from the Secession period. There's also a space dedicated to contemporary art (they hold 2 or 3 exhibitions a year). If you need a break, stop off in the gallery's small café.

❺ Anna Antikvitás – *D2* – *Falk Miksa utca 18–20* – Ⓜ *2 Kossuth Lajos tér,* 🚋 *2 Országház* – ☏ *(1) 302 5461* – *www.annaantikvitas.com* – *Mon–Fri 10am–6pm, Sat 10am–1am.* Pieces in bronze, hand-embroidered tablecloths, glass and porcelain items (1750–1940) are packed into this charming boutique. All hail from Austria, Hungary and the historic Transylvanian region. The prices are a little more affordable than in many similar shops in the street.

Vásárcsarnok

6 Kieselbach – *D2* – *Szent István körút 5* – 🚊 *4, 6 M. Jászai Mari tér* – *🖊 (1) 269 3148* – *www.kieselbach.hu* – *Mon–Fri 10am–6pm, Sat 10am–1pm.* This gallery, one of the most highly rated in Budapest, organises auction sales of paintings and photographs. Careful though, if you are tempted to bid, you might find the outcome a bit draining on the wallet.

Jewellery

30 ÜVEG/HÁZ – *D3* – *Sas utca 5* – Ⓜ *1 Bajcsy–Zsilinszky út* – *🖊 (30) 548 6376* – *www.uveghazbudapest.com* – *Daily except Sun, 11am–6pm.* This store specialises in elegant designer jewellery and accessories, including pieces made with coloured glass. Handmade items at reasonable prices.

ANDRÁSSY ÚT

Home and interior design

31 Goahome – *E5* – *Király utca 19* – Ⓜ *1 Opera* – *🖊 (70) 953 5620* – *www. goaworld.hu* – *Mon–Fri 10am–6pm, Sat 10am–2pm.* Vases, mirrors, ceramic tea bowls, glassware, stone figures, cushions and candlesticks, including many unique items, are dotted about this contemporary Ali Baba's cave with the slightest of oriental twists.

Confectionery

11 Sugar! – *E4* – *Paulay Ede utca 48* – Ⓜ *1 Opera* – *🖊 (1) 321 6672* – *www.sugarshop.hu* – *Tue–Sun 10.30am–10pm, Mon midday–10pm.* Giant lollipop trees, candy bars, colourful cupcakes and sugary gateaux, there's more than a touch of

Alice in Wonderland to this incredible confectioners. The bright colours of the sweets and candies stand out against the immaculate white of the walls and counters. Munch something sweet on the spot or buy some gifts to take home. The toilets are also worth a look, but we will leave you to discover exactly why.

BELVÁROS

Fashion and accessories

27 Paloma – *E6* – *Kossuth Lajos utca 14* – Ⓜ *3 Ferenciek tere* – *🖊 (20) 961 9160* – *palomabudapest. hu/en/home/* – *Mon–Fri 11am–7pm, Sat 11am–3pm.* Discover the work of some 40 or so young, up and coming Hungarian designers in this lovely old house built in 1894 by János Wagner, the founder of a prestigious Hungarian architectural dynasty. Today you can browse among unique pieces of jewellery, clothes, hats.... A dozen or so boutiques occupy two floors around a pretty courtyard, which sometimes also serves as the setting for various events.

Shoes

15 Vass Cipő – *D6* – *Haris köz 2* – Ⓜ *3 Ferenciek tere* – *🖊 (1) 318 2375* – *www.vass-shoes.hu* – *Mon–Fri 10am–7pm, Sat 10am–4pm.* This small shop sells fabulous handmade leather shoes for men. Some of the store's clients come here from abroad especially to have a pair or two made to measure.

Home and interior design

16 Herend Porcelain Manufactory – *D5* – *József Nádor tér 11* – Ⓜ *1, 2 or 3 Deák Ferenc tér* – ✆ *(20) 241 5736* – *www.herend.com* – *Mon–Fri 10am–6pm, Sat 10am–2pm.* This shop is the Budapest outlet for the famous Hungarian porcelain manufacturer Herend. Great ideas for quality gifts.

☺ **17 Holló Műhely** – *E5* – *Vitkovics Mihály utca 12* – Ⓜ *3 Ferenciek tere* – ✆ *(1) 317 8103* – *Mon–Fri 10am–1pm, 1.30pm–6pm, Sat 10am–2pm.* Founded in 1926, family-run Holló sells furniture and objects in wood decorated in traditional motifs from the Carpathian Basin. Beautiful painted eggs and boxes decorated with folk art motifs.

Design

☺ **18 Magma** – *D6* – *Petőfi Sándor utca 11* – Ⓜ *3 Ferenciek tere* – ✆ *(1) 235 0277* – *www.magma.hu* – *Mon–Fri 10am–7pm, Sat 10am–3pm.* This boutique-gallery gives Hungarian artists and designers the chance to show their wares: furniture, tableware (ceramics and porcelain), jewellery, (pretty rings in coloured glass), simple, elegant bags.

Gastronomy

28 Szamos Gourmet Ház – *D5* – *Váci utca 1* – Ⓜ *1 Vörösmarty tér* – ✆ *(30) 570 5973* – *www.szamos marcipan.hu* –*10am–9pm.* This excellent chocolatier is particularly known for its marzipan creations. A good place to buy gifts for the sweet-toothed or to sample something on the spot in the café, where they also serve breakfast and and snacks.

29 Paprika – *D5* – *Vörösmarty tér 1* – Ⓜ *1, 2 or 3 Deák Ferenc tér* – *www. paprikamarket.hu* – *10am–8pm (Fri & Sat 9pm).* The self-proclaimed 'biggest souvenir shop-market in Budapest'. Sachets of paprika, marzipan chocolates, Tokay wine, porcelain jewellery, embroidery…. A treasure trove for all things Hungarian for the dedicted souvenir hunter.

Music

20 Rózsavölgyi és Társa – *D5* – *Szervita tér 5* – Ⓜ *3 Ferenciek tere, 1 Vörösmarty tér* – ✆ *(1) 318 3500* – *www.rozsavolgyi.hu* – *10am–8pm except Sun.* One of the largest record stores in Budapest selling a wide range of classical and Hungarian folk music, among others.

ERZSÉBETVÁROS

97

Shoes

22 Tisza Cipő – *E5* – *Károly körút 1* – Ⓜ *2 Astoria* – ✆ *(1) 266 3055* – *www. tiszacipo.hu* – *Mon–Fri 10am–7pm, Sat 10am–4pm.* The place to find a pair of trainers or sneakers from this Hungarian manufacturer. They are all branded with the distinctive T logo.

Fashion

23 Retrock – *D5* – *Anker köz 2* – Ⓜ *1, 2 or 3 Deák Ferenc tér* – ✆ *(30) 472 3636* – *www.retrock.com* – *Mon–Thur 11am–9pm, Fri & Sat 11am–10pm, Sun 11am–8pm.* Specialising in vintage clothes and accessories, this vast shop is a favourite with Hungarian fashion followers, who like to browse through the collections from local designers.

🛍️

The prices are slightly higher than in similar shops in the area, but they reflect the more selective offering.

⑲ Ludovika – *E5* – Rumbach Sebestyén utca 15 – Ⓜ *1, 2 or 3 Deák Ferenc tér* – ℘ *(30) 718 3775* – *midday–8pm (Sat 6pm). Closed Sun.* Rummage through the rails at this quirky, fashionable shop for women. There's a selection of new and vintage clothes (jeans,blouses, jackets and dresses) along with accessories and trinkets.

Design, home accessories

㉔ Printa – *E5* – Rumbach Sebestyén utca 10 – Ⓜ *1, 2 or 3 Deák Ferenc tér* – ℘ *(30) 292 0329 – printa.hu – Daily except Sun, 11am–7pm.* This environmentally-conscious concept store, near Rumbach Street Synagogue, is art gallery, café and design store all in one. Decked out in black and white, it offers a good choice of silk screen prints and posters by emerging artists, and souvenirs, clothing and home accessories made from sustainable materials in limited editions. You'll be supporting young local designers and getting some cool souvenirs in one fell swoop.

FERENCVÁROS

Food

㉕ Vásárcsarnok (Central Market Hall) – *E7* – Vámház krt. 1–3 – Ⓜ *4* – 🚊 *2 Fővám tér – www.piaconline.hu – Mon 6am–5pm, Tue-Fri 6am–6pm, Sat 6am–3pm.* The famous indoor market is held in beautifully renovated halls that date from 1897. On the ground floor are many stalls selling traditional folklore products and food: strings of paprika, garlic and onions, wines and alcohol, and products from the ubiquitous famous Hungarian brand Pick. The upper floor gallery is full of stalls selling fast food and local crafts; they are great to browse through but just bear in mind that some verge on being 'tourist traps'.

Design

㉖ Flatlab – *E7* – Baross utca 3 – Ⓜ *3 or 4 Kálvin tér* – ℘ *(30) 949 4286 – www.flatlab.hu – Mon-Fri 1pm-8pm, Closed weekends.* Located near the Hungarian National Museum, this showroom in a minimalist apartment highlights pieces from young designers whose workshops are also on the premises (fashion, design and graphics). There's a range of things to buy – design items, gadgets and clothes – by local creators. A good place for ferreting out unique pieces or limited editions.

Alcohol

Zwack Unicum – *Off map* – Dandár utca 1 – 🚊 *2 Haller utca* – ℘ *(1) 456 5247 – unicum.hu – Mon-Fri 9am-6pm, Sat 10am-6pm.* Although the famous liqueur Unicum, made with 40 herbs, is sold just about everywhere, you might as well buy it directly from the distillery's shop and have a look around the small museum at the same time *(Mon-Sat 10am-5pm – Ft2,200 with audioguide and tasting).* Learn about Unicum's history, from 1790, when Dr Zwack first offered a sip to the king.

Printa

AWAY FROM THE CENTRE

Music
Ethno Sound – *Off map* – Komor Marcell utca 1 – HÉV 7 Közvágóhíd – 🚋 2 Millenniumi Kulturális Központ – ☏ (1) 555 3370 – ethnosound.hu – Mon–Fri 2pm–10pm, Sat & Sun 10am–10pm; closes 6pm on days when there are no evening performances. Musical instruments from all over the world (Tibet, India, Africa … you name it), from ocarinas to gongs, a treasure trove for music fans, especially for percussionists. You are welcome to try them out. Teaching materials and music therapy tools are also available.

Flea market
Ecseri piac – *Off map* – Nagykőrösi út 156 – from Boráros tér, bus 54, 55 to Használtcikk piac; from metro station 3 Határ út, bus 199 to Hofherr Albert utca – www.ecseripiac-budapest. hu/ – ☏ (1) 348 3200 – 8am–4pm, Sat 8am–3pm, Sun 8am–1pm. A flea market selling everything, just as it should do. It's one of the biggest in Central Europe. If you're looking for a one-off, you should be in luck, at least if you're into old phonographs, icons, medals and Red Army hats. Saturdays are best with lots of stalls to browse.

Nightlife

From opera to techno and of course folk music, Budapest offers a wide choice of shows and concerts, not to mention some that take place in more unusual venues for a fun evening out. For information, check the local press (**⚓** *p. 116),* hand-outs and the websites of the various venues. Some use ticket vendors such as those below, but you can often also buy tickets from venue box offices:

Ticket Express Hungary (TEX) – *E7* – *in Balná (p. 68) –* Ⓜ *4 Fővám tér,* Ⓣ *2 Zsil utca –* ☏ *(30) 505 0666 – www. eventim.hu – Mon–Fri 10am–6pm, Sat 11am–3pm.*

Ticket Pro – *D5* – *Károly krt. 9 –* Ⓜ *1, 2 or 3 Deák Ferenc tér –* ☏ *(1) 555 5515 – www.ticketpro.hu – Mon–Fri 10am–6pm, Sat 10am–2pm.* Tickets also available online.

Broadway Jegyiroda – *D2* – *Hollán Ernő utca 10 –* Ⓜ *3 Nyugati pályaudvar,* Ⓣ *4, 6 Jászai Mari tér –* ☏ *(1) 340 4040 – www.broadway.hu – Mon–Fri 10am–6pm. Closed public holidays.* Two venues not to miss in the Andrássy út district are the **Opera** and the **Academy of Music** (**⚓** *p. 101).* In the south of the city, the arts complex **MÜPA Budapest** offers a solid programme of theatre, dance and music (**⚓** *p. 104).* For something a little more lightweight, head for the Petőfi Bridge area, on the Buda side, where the **A38** cultural hub is moored(**⚓** *see right).* And don't forget a visit to a **romkocsma** (a 'ruin bar', one of the alternative bars and cafés set up in abandoned buildings in the Jewish district, such as **Szimpla Kert** (**⚓** *p. 102),* and in former factories and warehouses. See the website: ruinpubs.com.

Or try the lively high octane atmosphere of a **sparty**, one of the pool parties held on summer nights in the thermal pools. The latest tunes, irrepressible and energetic DJs, the water lit up by lights, giant screens and a strictly swimsuits dress code. The pool party scene comes to Central Europe! Tickets for the Széchenyi Baths sparty (**⚓** *p. 106)* summer season (June–Sept), or Lukács baths (**⚓** *p. 106)* winter season (Oct–May).

⚓ *Find the addresses on the detachable map (inside the cover) using the number in the listing (for example ❶). The coordinates in red (for example C2) refer to the same map.*

AROUND GELLÉRTHEGY

Music in the evening

❷ **Szatyor Bar** – *D8* – *Bartók B. út 36 –* Ⓜ *4,* Ⓣ *6 Móricz Zsigmond körtér (or* Ⓣ *19, 41, 47, 49, 56, 56A Gárdonyi tér) –* ☏ *(1) 279 0291 – www. szatyorbar.com – midday–1am (kitchen closes at 11pm).* A typically off-the-wall atmosphere that lends itself to long, late-night conversations. A good venue in which to see local bands from Budapest.

Live music, DJs

A38 – *Off map* – *Petőfi Bridge – a cargo ship moored on the Buda side of the river –* Tram *4, 6 Petőfi híd –* ☏ *(1) 464 3940 – www.a38.hu – 11am–4am.* Dance club, concert hall restaurant *(Mon–Sat 11am–11pm)* and cultural centre all rolled into one, this former Ukrainian cargo ship is one of the top spots in Budapest nightlife, with an eclectic programme of pop, rock, jazz and electro. Anchored on the Buda side, downstream from the Petőfi Bridge, the view across to Pest's east bank is lovely.

VÍZIVÁROS

Folklore

③ **Hagyományok háza (Hungarian Heritage House)** – *C4* – *Corvin tér 8 –* M *2 Batthyány tér –* ☏ *(1) 225 6049 – www.hagyomanyokhaza.hu – to book* ☏ *225 6056 (Mon–Thur midday–6pm, Fri 10am–2pm).* Performances by the talented musicians and dancers of the Hungarian State Folk Ensemble, which was founded in 1951.

LIPÓTVÁROS

Club

④ **Morrison's 2** – *D2* – *Szent István krt 11 –* Tram *4, 6 Jászai Mari tér –* ☏ *(1) 374 3329 – www.morrisons.hu – 5pm–6am.* A buzzing music-bar venue: 10 bars, 6 dance floors, table football, karaoke – it's a party every night. The inner courtyard is under cover and heated. Sports events are broadcast on a giant screen.

Folk music

⑤ **Duna Palota** – *D4* – *Zrínyi utca 5 –* M *1, 2 or 3 Deák Ferenc tér –* ☏ *(1) 235 5500 – www.dunapalota.hu.* Duna Palota translates as the Danube Palace, an elegant and intimate venue. The shows start at 8pm, alternating between three internationally renowned folk ensembles. You can also opt to take a Danube dinner-cruise after the show.

Jazz

⑦ **Budapest Jazz Club** – *D2* – *Hollán Ernő utca 7 –* M *3 Nyugati pályaudvar,* Tram *4, 6 Jászai Mari tér –* ☏ *(1) 413 9837 –* ☏ *(1) 798 7289 – www.bjc.hu – Sun–Thur 10am–midnight, Fri–Sat 10am–2pm.* The most famous jazz club in Budapest offers live concerts every day, by famous musicians or students, depending on the programme. Enjoy the music, with a glass of excellent wine in hand if you so choose.

ANDRÁSSY ÚT

Classical music

⑧ **Magyar Állami Operaház (Hungarian State Opera House)** – *E4* – *Andrássy út 22 –* M *1 Opera –* ☏ *(1) 332 7914 – www.opera.hu.* One of the most prestigious opera houses in Europe with performances in a neo-Renaissance palace (1884), adorned by frescoes painted by the greatest Hungarian artists of the time. The biggest names in music play here. Closed for restoration until around 2020, performances take place at the Erkel Theatre and other venues.

101

🎵 **⑩ Liszt Ferenc Zeneművészeti Egyetem (Franz Liszt Academy of Music)** – *E4* – *Liszt Ferenc tér 8* – Ⓜ *1 Oktogon* – ✆ *(1) 321 0690* – *zeneakademia.hu*. Founded by the eponymous Hungarian composer in 1907, the academy remains the capital's premier concert venue. It occupies a beautiful Art Nouveau building with stained-glass windows, mosaics and sparkling crystal chandeliers. Audiences will be rewarded with performances by the best symphony orchestras in the country at very affordable prices. And if you're nearby at rehearsal time, you can often hear strains of music echoing through the neighbourhood.

Puppets

⑨ Bábszínház (Budapest Puppet Theatre) – *F3* – *Andrássy út 69* – Ⓜ *1 Oktogon* – ✆ *(1) 321 5200* – *www.budapest-babszinhaz.hu* – *reservation 9am–6pm*. A very well known puppet theatre for children and adults. Some performances are adaptations of works by the likes of Mozart, Bartók.

Aperitifs with a view

⑪ 360 Bar – *E4* – *Andrássy út 39* – Ⓜ *1 Opera* – ✆ *(30) 356 3047* – *360bar.hu* – *Mon–Wed 2pm–midnight, Thur–Sat 2pm–2am, Sun midday–midnight*. Budapest's most beautiful rooftop bar, on top of the old Párizsi Nagyáruház department store. It's the perfect spot for an aperitif while watching the sun go down. You can still do so in winter and enjoy the same views, but cocooned safely inside one of the eight transparent domes in the Igloo Garden.

Cocktails

⑫ Boutiq'Bar – *D5* – *Paulay Ede utca 5* – Ⓜ *1 Bajcsy-Zsilinszky út* – ✆ *(30) 554 2323* – *www.boutiqbar.hu* – *Tue–Thur 6pm–1am, Fri–Sat 6pm–2am*. Some people swear that you will find the best cocktails in Budapest here. Most are house specials, but the bartenders will still willingly prepare the great classics for you, from daiquiris to cosmopolitans.

ERZSÉBERTVÁROS

Ruin bar

⑭ Szimpla Kert – *E5* – *Kazinczy utca 14* – Ⓜ *2 Astoria* – ✆ *(20) 261 8669* – *szimpla.hu* – *Mon–Sat midday–4am, Sun 9pm–4am*. Reclaimed furniture, exposed pipes and ducting, lit by small colored lamps, a pretty courtyard ... this is a genuine *romkocsma*. Szimpla Kert is an institution, but go for a drink and the music rather than to eat. DJ's and live music (from 8pm) in the evening.

⑯ Ellátó Kert – *E5* – *Kazinczy utca 48* – Ⓜ *1, 2 or 3 Deák Ferenc tér* – ✆ *(20) 527 3018* – *Mon–Wed 5pm–2pm, Thur–Fri 5pm–4am, Sat 6pm–4am, Sun 6pm–2am*. It's a little bit touristy here, but the decor is 100% upcycled, with colourful walls and tables. Try a beer on the pleasant patio (heated in winter). Excellent Mexican-inspired tapas prepared in front of you. DJs and live music at the weekends. The prices are reasonable.

Szimpla Kert

Wine tasting

15 **Doblo Wine & Bar** – *E5* – *Dob utca 20* – **M** *2 Astoria* – *(20) 398 8863* – *www.budapestwine.com* – *Mon–Wed & Sun 2pm–2am, Thur–Sat 2pm–4am.* This dynamic wine bar is an excellent place to start discovering the charms of Hungary as a wine-growing country, such as sweet Tokay or fruity red wines from Szekszárd. Oenophiles will relish the range of wines on offer, served against a backdrop of brick walls and bottles of wine warmly lit by lamps.

MARGITSZIGET

Shows & concerts

Margitsziget Open-air Theatre – *Off map* – Bus 26: Szabadtéri színpad – *(1) 375 5922* – *www.szabadter.hu.* Performances at the open-air theatre on Margaret Island during the summer, including theatre, dance and opera. The Budapest Summer Festival (http://eng.szabadter.hu/), a celebration of music and dance, takes place at several venues on the island, including the amazing Art Nouveau Margaret Island Water Tower.

AWAY FROM THE CENTRE

Shows & concerts

MÜPA Budapest – *Off map* – Komor Marcell utca 1 – HÉV 7 – **Tram** 1 Közvágóhíd – *(1) 555 3000* – *www.mupa.hu* – *10am–10pm* – *end June to end Aug.* This cultural arts complex has been offering a very varied programme of excellent quality since it opened in 2005

Müpa Budapest

© Hungarian Tourism Agency

(opera, contemporary dance, jazz, world music, classical and contemporary music, films….). Artists of an international standing play here as does the Hungarian National Philharmonic Orchestra. Free concerts are on offer several times a week, performed by students of the Conservatory of Music. There is also a programme of live broadcast performances from New York's Metropolitan Opera (in the original language with Hungarian subtitles). The Müpa building includes the Béla Bartók National Concert Hall, the Ludwig Museum of Contemporary Arts (*p. 68*) along with the Festival Theatre.

Visiting the baths

Going to the baths is very much an institution in Budapest. They are particularly busy at weekends when families swell the numbers of people enjoying them. They are managed by BGYH. See **www.spasbudapest.com** *(in English)* for details on a dozen baths, including their location and information on the different pools, water temperature and prices. See **www.bathsbudapest.com** for *sparty* (🕯 *p. 100*), the pool parties that are organized at weekends.

Prices

Entrance to the baths is cheaper on **weekdays** than at weekends, and some baths offer a reduced rate at the end of the day. The prices given here are for the minimum daily rate, but some baths also offer half-day rates. ☺ A 20% reduction on the entrance fee to some baths with the **Budapest Card** (🕯 *p. 114*). Some baths do not accept credit cards. Take cash with you, especially if you plan to have a treatment (allow Ft6,000 for a 20-min massage). You can normally choose between the cabin rate (changing rooms where you can leave your belongings safely) or the cheaper locker rate (storage only, get changed in communal men-/women-only changing rooms). You will be given a wristband or an electronic card to unlock and lock your locker. The prices given here are for adults. If you have children with you, enquire beforehand as some baths refuse entry to those under 14 years.

OUR PICK OF THE BATHS

🕯*Find the addresses on the detachable map (inside the cover) using the number in the listing (for example ①). The coordinates in red (for example C2) refer to the same map.*

😊 ① **Gellért Baths** – *D8* – *Kelenhegyi út 4 – Entrance in the street to the right of the hotel –* Ⓜ *4,* 🚊 *19, 41, 47, 48, 49, 56, 56A Szent Gellért tér –* 🕿 *(1) 466 6166 – fr.gellertfurdo.hu – 6am–8pm – mixed baths – from Ft5,600.* They might be in need of a little refurbishment, but the Gellért Baths (12 pools in all) are some of the most spectacular in the capital with beautiful Art Nouveau design. First discovered in the 15C, they opened in 1918. The complex includes a 'resort' section (pool with wave machine, solarium, sauna, bar, eateries, beautiful indoor pool) and a thermal baths section (two baths at 36/38 °C, a cold bath, saunas, steam room). Massages are available and there's a VIP spa. The thermal waters are said to be particularly good for easing rheumatism and osteoarthritis. 🕯 *See also p. 31.*

② **Rudas Baths** – *D6* – *Döbrentei tér 9 –* 🚊 *19, 41, 56, 56A Rudas Gyógyfürdő –* 🕿 *(1) 356 1322 – fr.rudasfurdo.hu – Women only Tue; men only Mon & Wed-Fri; mixed at the weekend – Opening times: Mon-Thur & Sun 6am-8pm; Fri-Sat 10pm-4am – from Ft3,500.* This authentic Turkish

105

bath, one of the oldest in the city (built in the 16C), includes a thermal bath (water at 16–42°C) and a separate interior swimming pool (29°C). A number of different types of massage are available (firming, aroma, exfoliating, relaxing...). *See also p. 32.*

③ Király Baths – *C3* – Fő utca 84 – **Ⓜ** 2 Batthyány tér, **Tram** 19, 41 Bem József tér – *℘ (1) 202 3688 – fr.kiralyfurdo. hu – Mixed baths – 9am–9pm – from Ft2,500.* These medieval Turkish baths are very atmospheric, with shafts of light penetrating through holes in the dome over the octagonal pool (36°C), just as they have done for centuries. The baths are thermal and are indoors only: they include, a hamam and a sauna. Massages and pedicures are also available. *See also p. 36.*

④ Lukács Baths – *C1* – Frankel Leó út 25–29 – **Tram** 17, 19, 41 Szent Lukács Gyógyfürdő – *℘ (1) 326 1695 – fr.lukacsfurdo.hu – Mixed baths – 6am–10pm – from Ft3,700.* With a regular clientele of locals and people taking a cure, the Lukács Baths tend to have fewer tourists than others. Renovated in 2012, they include 2 outdoor pools, a sundeck and outdoor fitness equipment. Inside there are 5 thermal pools (22–40°C) and the newly opened 'sauna world' *(Ft500 extra)* with an infrared sauna, Himalayan salt wall and ice machines. *See also p. 72.*

😊 ⑤ Széchenyi Baths – *G1* – Állatkerti körút 11 – **Ⓜ** 1 Széchenyi fürdő – *℘ (1) 363 3210 – fr.szechenyifurdo.hu – Mixed baths – 6am–10pm – from Ft5,200.*

In the heart of Városliget (City Park). Outside you'll find a thermal whirlpool, an Olympic sized swimming pool, a thermal pool (38 °C), solarium and restaurant. Inside there are several baths, from cold to very warm. Treatments and massages are provided in booths. *See also p. 55.*

Veli Bej Baths – *C1* – Árpád Fejedelem útja 7 – **Tram** 17, 19, 41 Komjádi Béla utca – *℘ (1) 438 8587 – www.irgalmasrend.hu – Mixed baths – 6am–midday, 3pm–9pm – from Ft2,500.* The largest Turkish baths in Budapest with 5 pools (central pool 36–38 °C). Steams baths with aromatic oils, sauna, jacuzzi, swimming pool, jet massage. Massages can be booked at the entrance. Café accessible from the baths.

Dandár Baths – *Off map* – Dandár utca 5–7 – **Tram** 2, 24 Haller utca/ Soroksári út – *℘ (1) 215 7084 – en.dandarfurdo.hu – Mixed baths – 6am–9pm, weekend 8am–9pm – from Ft1,900.* These indoor thermal baths (20–38°C) underwent a complete refurbishment in 2014. Saunas and massages are also available.

Palatinus Strand Baths – *Off map* – Margitsziget – **Bus** 26 – *℘ (1) 340 4500 - en.palatinusstrand.hu – May-Aug 9am–8pm – from Ft3,100.* The largest open-air bathing complex in Budapest, on Margaret Island, with 11 pools (one with waves), a slide park and a beach. The water is at 22–36°C. Four new indoor pools are now open all year round. Next door are some tennis courts and there are also football and beach volleyball pitches nearby on the island. *See also p. 71.*

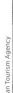

© Hungarian Tourism Agency

Király Baths

TIPS FOR HAPPY BATHING

Start by choosing your dates: although many baths are mixed, some still work on the basis of timed slots for either men or women. Many people don't bother with a swimsuit when it's single sex, so it's up to you. Remember to take your swimsuit and a towel (and/or a bathrobe) and a pair of flip-flops; you may also be able to hire these on site but they can be expensive. You usually need a swimming cap for the swimming pools (you may be able to buy one at the baths). A plastic bag is useful for carrying your toiletries about (shampoo, soap, brush or comb), not to mention a soggy swimsuit when you are ready to leave. Hairdryers are usually available in the changing rooms.Inside the baths, you can usually choose between several pools: the thermal pools and the swimming pools. Some baths also have saunas and steam rooms and most have facilities offering light meals and drinks as well as different therapeutic treatments.For the complete bathing experience, book a massage upon arrival at the entrance (or in advance via the website if possible). Don't leave the baths without spending some time in the rest rooms to allow your body to adapt to the ambient temperature gradually. It is particularly important in winter when the north winds can prevail.

Where to stay

Most of Budapest's hotels are at the higher end of the market price-wise and it is not always easy to find cheap rooms in the city centre, although things are changing. Renting an apartment, even for one night, is very common (www.7seasonsapartments.com or www.only-apartments.com), and can be a useful alternative. Or try one of the websites offering homestay accommodation (Booking.com, Airbnb, etc.).

Which side of the river? On the Buda side (west bank), the atmosphere is more relaxed and peaceful, with lovely views of the Danube. The city centre is on the far busier Pest side.

Prices – The rates given here are the minimum for a double room in high season, bearing in mind that prices can rise during the holidays and when the Formula 1 Grand Prix is in town (late July–early Aug). You can also find discounted rates on the Internet.

Find the addresses on the detachable map (inside the cover) using the number in the listing (for example 1). The coordinates in red (for example D2) refer to the same map.

VÁRNEGYED

Ft38,880–58,320

😊 **12** **Baltazár** – *B4* – *Országház utca 31* – 🚌 *16, 16A, 116 Bécsi kapu tér*, Ⓜ *2 Széll Kálmán tér* – ☎ *(1) 300 7051* – *baltazarbudapest.com – 11 rooms.*

A charming boutique hotel, with very comfortable rooms, all decorated differently. The atmosphere is calm and there is an excellent restaurant with a terrace and a nice wine bar.

VÍZIVÁROS

Ft38,880–58,320

2 **Victoria** – *C4* – *Bem Rakpart 11* – Ⓜ *2 Batthyány tér*, 🚊 *19, 41 Halász utca* – ☎ *(1) 457 8080* – *www.victoria.hu – 27 rooms.* 🛏 *included.* A peaceful and charming hotel with tastefully decorated and well-appointed rooms. Situated near the castle, there are great views of the Danube.

3 **Art'otel** – *C4* – *Bem Rakpart 16–19* – Ⓜ *2 Batthyány tér*, 🚊 *19, 41 Halász utca* – ☎ *(1) 487 9487* – *www.artotels.com – 156 rooms.* 🛏 *included* – 🍴. Situated by the river, near the castle and the commercial district of the city centre, this chic hotel lives up to its name by displaying the work of American artist Donald Sultan. Views of the Parliament Building and the Chain Bridge, beautiful lit up at night.

LIPÓTVÁROS

Ft38,880–58,320

4 **Central Basilica** – *D4* – *Hercegprímás utca 8* – Ⓜ *1 Bajcsy-Zsilinsky út* – ☎ *(1) 328 5010* – *www.hotelcentral-basilica.hu* –

37 rooms. – ☞ included. Located in the historic centre, near the basilica, this hotel represents good value for money. It has elegant rooms and several apartments for families.

BELVÁROS

Ft22,680–38,880

8 **Leo Panzió – D6** – *Kossuth Lajos utca 2/a* – Ⓜ *3 Ferenciek tere* – *☎ (1) 266 9041 – www.leopanzio.hu – 14 rooms. ☞ included.* In an elegant but slightly dated turn-of-the-century building, this small yet well-kept hotel has a contemporary interior and is located in the city centre. Comfortable and good value for money, but the street is rather busy.

9 **Gerlóczy Kávéház – Rooms de Lux – E5** – *V. Gerlóczy utca 1* – Ⓜ *3 Ferenciek tere,* Ⓜ *2 Astoria* – *☎ (1) 501 4000 – www.gerloczy. hu – 19 rooms. –* ✗. Just a few steps from the River Danube, this tiny hotel, with a café annex is very belle époque in ambience. It manages to reconcile retro charm and attention to detail with modern comfort.

ERZSÉBETVÁROS

Under Ft22,680

5 **Wombat Hostel – E5** – *Király utca 20* – Ⓜ *1 Bajcsy–Zsilinsky út* – *☎ (1) 883 5005 – www.wombats-hostels.com – 112 rooms and dormitories.* A good example of youth hostel-style accommodation, but a little more designer-led than is usual. Previously a four-star hotel, the rooms and dormitories are spotless. Good for

those on a budget despite sometimes being a bit noisy.

Ft22,680–38,880

1 **Roombach – E5** – *Rumbach Sebestyén utca 14* – Ⓜ *1, 2 or 3 Deák Ferenc tér* – *☎ (1) 413 0253 – roombach.accenthotels.com – 98 rooms. ☞ included.* Ideally located in the heart of the most hyped district of the capital, you can walk from here on foot to the city's major sites. The rooms are small but comfortable and spotless. A friendly welcome and a varied buffet-style breakfast.

6 **Seven Seasons Apartments – D5** – *Kiraly utca 8* – Ⓜ *1, 2 or 3 Deák Ferenc tér* – *☎ (20) 274 7777 – www.7seasonsapartments.com – 40 apartments, from studios to 3-bed apartments.* The building may be rather impersonal, but its central location and clean and simple apartments make it an ideal base from which to explore the city.

Over Ft58,320

7 **Corinthia Hotel – F4** – *Erzsébet körút 43–49* – Ⓜ *1 Oktogon,* 🚊 *4, 6 Király utca* – *☎ (1) 479 4000 – www. corinthia.com –* ⚊ *– 383 rooms –* ✗ *Bock Bisztró.* This legendary hotel dating from 1896 has been completely renovated. Up until the Second World War it was *the* place to stay in Budapest. Its elegant belle époque-style façade now conceals a contemporary interior that plays the luxury card effortlessly, with light-filled atriums, wide corridors and well-appointed rooms. There is also a spa and leisure centre offering treatments.
👆*See also 'Where to eat' p. 88.*

109

Planning your trip

Buda Castle and the Danube
© Hungarian Tourism Agency

Know before you go

ENTRY REQUIREMENTS

ID documents: A passport is required for travel. Check your passport validity and visa requirements at www.gov.uk. Check with the Hungarian Embassy in London for longer stays https://london.mfa.gov.hu/eng. US citizens may enter Hungary for up to 90 days for tourist or business purposes without a visa. Your US passport should be valid for at least three months beyond the period of stay. Carry your passport at all times. You must be able to show some form of ID when requested, a photocopy is not acceptable.

BY PLANE

There is just one airport, **Budapest Ferenc Liszt** (🦽 *p. 3*).
Budapest and the UK are very well connected, with various airlines flying direct daily to the Hungarian capital; flights from the US generally involve a transfer:

British Airways: www.britishairways.com, from London Heathrow.
Norwegian Air: www.norwegian.com, from London Gatwick
Budget airlines
EasyJet: www.easyjet.com, from London Gatwick.
Ryanair: www.ryanair.com, from London Stansted, East Midlands, Bristol and Manchester.
Wizz Air: www.wizzair.com, from Birmingham, Liverpool, Luton.

Jet2: www.jet2.com, from Manchester, Edinburgh, Leeds, East Midlands.
Norwegian Air: www.norwegian.com, from London Gatwick.
From Dublin: Ryanair and Aer Lingus offer direct flights.
From the US: there are no direct flights from the US.
From Canada: direct flights are available with Air Canada.

BY TRAIN/COACH

Budapest has three international railway stations and is well connected with nearby European capitals such as Vienna and Bratislava. The train journey from London to Budapest takes around 24hr (by Eurostar to Paris, TGV from Paris to Munich, overnight sleeper to Budapest). The international bus station is located in Népliget (10th district Üllői út 131). You can book tickets online at: www.volanbusz.hu/en.

LEFT LUGGAGE

The website **luggagepals.com** allows you to pay online (small bag €5 a day, large €6) and leave your luggage with a business or café in Budapest.

MONEY

Currrency: The local currency is the Forint (abbreviated to Ft locally and HUF internationally).

Euro: Hungary is preparing to adopt the euro. Some prices are shown in euros, in particular hotel rooms. However, the exchange rate in hotels is generally unfavourable so if you want to consider settling the bill in cash in euros, you might want to exchange them first elsewhere.

Conversion: Change currency in banks, bureaux de change, travel agents, hotels and airports; there are automatic cashpoints near the baggage collection in the airport but the exchange rate is unfavourable. Never change currency with street vendors offering attractive rates. It is an illegal practice and the risk of scamming is high (⚫ *Banks p. 114*).

Credit cards: Payment by credit card is common; the following are generally accepted: Diners Club, Cirrus, American Express, Euro/MasterCard, JCB and Visa.

ATMS: Look out for the Bankomat sign. There are lots of cashpoints in the city and instructions are in several languages, German and English in particular.

Customs: Hungary is a member of the European Union. Due to the Schengen Agreement, there are no contols within the EU. If arriving from outside the EU, you will need to pass through customs and declare goods.

SEASONS

Hungary has a continental climate, with very warm summers, during which temperatures can exceed 30°C in July and August, and cold winters when daytime temperatures regularly fall below zero, particularly in January. Spring and autumn are the most pleasant seasons in the capital.
⚫ Hotels are often full for key events.

TOURIST INFORMATION

Useful information

Budapest's official tourist website is **www.budapestinfo.hu**. Hungary's official tourist website is **hellohungary.com**, while **welovebudapest.com** offers useful information on bars, restaurants, shopping, nightlife, etc. Helpful addresses and inside information are also available on **spottedbylocals.com**.

Local information

Tourinform offices (tourinform.hu) provide visitors with information on places to see, accommodation, restaurants, spas, etc.
⚫ Copies of the tourist office's publication **Budapest Guide** (along with maps of Budapest) are available free of charge in several languages.

Tourinform Office Sütő utca – Sütő utca 2 (Belváros, near Deák Ferenc – **D5**), 8am–8pm.

Tourinform Office Airport: Terminal 2A, 8am–10pm and Terminal 2B, 10am–10pm.

Tourinform Call Centre ☎ (1) 438 8080 7am–7pm (in English).
⚫ In the busy visitor season mobile information kiosks are located in the key tourist areas.

Basic information

BANKS

Commission and exchange rates: The bureaux de change in the city centre and at railway stations normally offer the best rates, but watch out for hidden charges. The banks charge average rates of commission but in hotels and at the airport commission is usually much higher. This can make ATMs a better bet, but check what fees your bank charges to withdraw cash from them before you travel.

Currency: Bank notes are available in the following denominations: Ft500, 1,000, 2,000, 5,000, 10,000 and Ft20,000. Coins are worth Ft5, 10, 20, 50, 100 and Ft200. Make sure you check the number of zeros on coins and notes when handing over or receiving them – it's easy to make a mistake in a foreign currency and, as everywhere, there are some dishonest folk in Budapest too.
Opening hours, p.116.

BUDAPEST CARD

It makes sense to invest in a Budapest Kártya/Budapest Card (for 48 or 72 hr) if you plan to visit museums and want to enjoy unrestricted travel on public transport within the city boundaries. (When travelling outside them, you must buy an extension ticket from your departure point while presenting your Budapest Card, *Transport tickets p. 117.*) The benefits include:

– Free unlimited travel on the public transport system (BKV), including metro, bus, trolley buses, trams, HÉV suburban trains, but excluding both the Buda Funicular (*p. 14 Sikló*) and the chair lift (*p. 76 Libegő*).
–Free entry (or reduced price) in a number of musuems and cultural attractions.
– Discounts on tickets for certain shows, in some shops, restaurants, cafés, pubs and thermal baths.
– Discounts at some car hire firms and for bike hire on Margaret Island (Margitsziget).
You can buy the Budapest Card at the airport, in Tourinform offices (*p. 113*), in the major metro stations, travel agents and online at budapest-card.com, with a 5 per cent discount.
Prices: as follows. Once you have purchased your card, make sure you sign and date it. A small explanatory booklet accompanies the card.
24hr F6,490/€21.99,
48hr Ft9,990/€32.99,
72hr Ft12,990/€42.99,
96hr Ft15,900/€54.

CYCLING

Cars are not allowed on Margaret Island, which makes it the perfect place to stretch your legs. You can hire bikes on arrival or enjoy a guided tour by bike. *Opposite page.*
The **bike sharing network** MOL Bubi (molbubi.bkk.hu) hires out green bikes at certain locations, mostly on

the Pest side. 24hr hire costs Ft500, 72hr costs Ft1,000 and Ft2,000 for a week.

ELECTRICITY

The voltage is 220 volts, as in continental Europe.

EMBASSIES

British Embassy: Füge utca 5–7 – ℰ (1) 266 2888 – www. gov.uk/world/organisations/ british-embassy-budapest
US Embassy: Szabadság tér – ℰ (1) 475 4400 – hu.usembassy.gov/
Embassy of Canada: Ganz utca 12–14 – ℰ (1) 392 3360 – www.canadainternational.gc.ca/ hungary-hongrie/
Embassy of Ireland: Szabadság tér 7 ℰ (1) 301 4960 – www.dfa.ie/ irish-embassy/hungary/
Australian Embassy: closed. Enquiries can be directed to the Australian Embassy in Vienna – ℰ+43 1 506 740 – austria.embassy.gov.au.

GUIDED TOURS

A number of companies offer walking tours, some themed. Information is available from Tourinform (♿ *p. 113*). Some companies quote their prices in euros.

Walking, segway & cycle tours
Absolute Tours: ℰ (1) 269 3843 – www.absolutetours.com. Offers 3-hour themed walks for around €36, along with cycle and Segway tours.

(♿ *p. 113*)

Emergency numbers
European emergency number: ℰ 112
Ambulance: ℰ 104
Police: ℰ 107
Fire service: ℰ 105
24hr doctor (Főnix SOS): ℰ (1) 203–3615
24hr chemist: Teréz Patika – Teréz krt. 41 (***E3***) – ℰ (1) 311 443
Emergency dentist: ℰ (1) 317 6600

Yellow Zebra Bikes: Sütő utca 2 – Ⓜ 1, 2 or 3 Deák Ferenc tér – ℰ (1) 269 3843 – From around €28 for 4 hours including a café stop.

Bike and electric bike tours.
BudaBike Tours: ℰ (1) 70 242 5736 – www.budabike.com – Book ahead. Offers 5 tours of the city for 2/3 hours at €25/30, including a night tour.

Bus tours
Big Bus Tours: Andrássy út 3 – Ⓜ 1 Bajcsy–Zsilinszky út – ℰ 235 0078 – eng.bigbustours.com. Double-decker buses with multilingual audioguides and a choice of 26 stops, hop-on & hop-off (price reduction with the Budapest Card).
A 2-day pass starts at around €24.30.
City Tour: Andrássy út 2 – Ⓜ 1 Bajcsy–Zsilinszky út – ℰ 374 7073 – www.citytour.hu. Operates like the Big Bus with a reduction on price with the Budapest Card.
A 2-day pass starts at €24.
Cityrama: Báthory utca 22 – ℰ 302 4382 – www.cityrama.hu. 3-hour tours start at €25.

Floating bus
RiverRide: Széchenyi tér – ℰ 332 2555 – riverride.com. An amphibious

vehicle that takes you through the city and then onto the river Danube! Prices start at Ft9,000.

Boat trips

See the riverfront sights in Buda and Pest from aboard a boat on the Danube. Choose between a daytime tour with multilingual commentary, or an evening tour with a dinner or a concert.

Legenda: Departures from quay 7 – Vigadó tér – Ⓜ 1 Vörösmarty tér – 🚋 2 Vigadó tér – 📞 (1) 317 2203 – www.legenda.hu. Daytime 70-min cruise starts at Ft3,900.

Mahart PassNave: Belgrád rakpart – Ⓜ 4 Fővám tér – 🚋 2 Fővám tér – 📞 (1) 484 4013 – www.mahart passnave.hu. Dinner starts at Ft10,900 (reduction with the Budapest Card).

Trabant tour

Cityrama: ♿ *Bus tours p.115.* See previous entry for details. 3-hr trip leaving at 10.30am from the Cityrama office or your hotel (if you are based in the city centre), with or without an English- speaking driver. You will need to show your driving licence if you want to drive yourself. A private tour for 2 will cost around €120.

NEWSPAPERS AND MAGAZINES

You will find English-language magazines and newspapers in the city centre and in many hotels. *The Budapest Times* (www.budapest times.hu) is an independent weekly English-language newspaper featuring articles on business, politics, culture and health.

Budapest's Finest, an English-language quarterly magazine is available from Tourinform offices and most hotels. Access it online at www. budapestinfo.hu/budapests-finest. It highlights the best that Budapest has to offer in terms of cultural activities, museums, shops and restaurants. The monthly *Budapest Funzine* (www. budapestfunzine.hu) is also full of useful information on cultural activities and entertainment in the city and the latest events.

OPENING HOURS

Shops: Mon–Fri 10am–6pm (Sat 2pm). Some shops and stores stay open on Saturday afternoons and on Sunday, particularly those in the shopping centres and key tourist locations, including near the castle and on Váci utca. Food shops are often open 7am–7pm (Sat 2pm) and 24-hr food stores usually display the sign 'Non Stop'.
🈺 Most shops are closed 26 December.
Banks: Mon–Thur 8am–5pm; Fri 8am–2pm.
Museums and monuments: 10am–6pm (some close Mon and public holidays).
Post offices: Mon–Fri 8am–6pm, Sat 8am–12pm. In Pest (***E3***): Teréz krt. 51, 7am–8pm, Sun 8am–6pm.

PHOTOGRAPHY/FILMING

Be aware that if you want to take photographs or film clips in museums, you must pay (between Ft500 and Ft2,000).

POST

Post boxes are usually red with a hunting horn emblem. Stamps (*bélyeg*) are sold in post offices and some newsagents. A postcard takes 3–8 days to reach continental Europe; a postcard stamp for delivery within the EU costs Ft370.

PUBLIC HOLIDAYS

– 1 January (New Year's Day)
– 15 March (national holiday commemorating the Revolution of 1848–1849)
– Good Friday, Easter Sunday and Easter Monday
– 1 May (Labour Day)
– Pentecost/Whit Monday
– 20 August (St Stephen's Day and Constitution Day, ⚓ *p. 30*)
– 23 October (Day of the Republic, commemorating the revolution of 1956)
– 1 November (All Saints' Day)
– 25 and 26 December Christmas

PUBLIC TRANSPORT

Budapest has a very efficient public transport system operated by BKK. You can access timetables and maps at **www.bkk.hu/en**. Buses, trams and trolley buses generally operate between 4.30am and 11pm. Night buses run outside these hours. The metro operates until 11.30pm (M2 & M4 – Fri & Sat until 0.30am). M3 is partially closed for reconstruction, metro replacement buses and trams are operating.

Key transport hubs:
– In Buda: Batthyány tér and Széll Kálmán tér.
– In Pest: Deák F. tér and Blaha L. tér.
⚓ The nearest metro station or tram stop to a venue is indicated in the guide. The metro and tram are also generally the easiest ways to get about in the city.
⚓ *Getting to Budapest p. 3 and the public transport map on the reverse of the detachable map.*

Transport tickets

A **single ticket** (valid on the metro, buses, trams or trolley buses and HÉV trains within the city) costs Ft350 and a book of 10 Ft3,000. Tickets can be bought at the airport, metro stations, train stations, some newspaper kiosks and vending machines at transport stops. And also from BKK (Centre for Budapest Transport) counters in the major transport hubs and terminuses You cannot buy tickets on the trams or trolley buses, but you can buy them from bus drivers (Ft450).
You must **validate** tickets before travel. **Metro:** look for the machines at the entrance to metro stations and the (white) boundary line (you may be fined if you cross this without a ticket). You can use the same single ticket on the metro for any number of changes for up to 80 minutes from validation, but you cannot exit a station and return on the same ticket.
Trams, **trolleybuses**, **buses**, **suburban railway trains**: the validating machines are by the doors on board the vehicle.
To change between types of transport using one ticket (bus, tram, metro and trolley bus), buy a **transfer ticket**

(Ft530). Transfer tickets must be validated each time you board: first when starting a trip at one end, and at the other end when transferring, apart from on the metro. They are valid for 100 mins from the first validation and 80 mins from the second. Travelcards are the **best value** for **limitless travel** within the boundaries of Budapest: 1 day (Ft1,650), 3 days (Ft4,150) and 7 days (Ft4,950).

The transport ticket tariffs and regulations are quite complicated, more info. is available at: bkk.hu/en/tickets-and-passes/.

Budapest Card p. 114.

As a reminder of the socialist era, Hungarian and now EU seniors (over 65) can travel free on public transport on presentation of a valid form of ID.

Metro

The 4 lines in Budapest (M1, M2, M3 and M4) are differentiated by colour: M1 yellow, M2 red, M3 blue and M4 green. M1 (known locally as Kisföldalatti or 'small underground') was the first underground railway in continental Europe and follows Andrássy út above ground, linking the city centre to City Park (Városliget). Opened in 2014 and ultra modern, line M4 links Gellért in the south to Keleti Pályaudvar in the north. Lines 1, 2 and 3 all pass through Deák Ferenc tér. Doors open and close automatically and the name of the next stop is announced in the carriage. Inspections are made regularly and inspectors wear red armbands rather than a uniform. Ask for a receipt if you are given a fine.

Two signs you need to know: *bejárat* (entrance) and *kijárat* (exit). The different metro lines are indicated by colour and destination on each platform. Some stations are at very deep levels, so the escalators can be steep, not to mention speedy. Take care in busy times when there can be quite a crush.

Buses and trolley buses

Buses are blue and trolley buses red. Buses with a black number stop at all stops and those with a red number or the letter 'E' are express buses which skip some. Each stop is labelled with its name and times are given on the blue signs (generally between 5 and 15 minutes depending on the time of day). Stops are sometimes announced. Push the button near the door to signal that you want to get off, particularly in the evening or later.

Tramways (Villamos)

Tram carriages are yellow (with a couple of exceptions) and travel the length and breadth of the city. Stops are sometimes announced. There are two night lines. The lines serving the most popular tourist areas are:
– **4** and **6:** runs along the Grand Boulevard to Széll Kálmán tér;
– **2:** runs along the Danube on the Pest side from Közvágóhíd to Jászai Mari tér (near the bridge and Margaret Island);
– **19:** runs along the Danube on the Buda side to Batthyöny tér.
– **60:** the Cog Railway (**Fogaskerekű**, also designated tram 60) is very well used by the locals, and links Városmajor with the Buda Hills.

Spice of Europe
BUDAPEST
LET US SHOW YOU
THE SPICE OF LIFE.
WWW.SPICEOFEUROPE.COM
spiceofeurope
Spice of Europe
@spiceofeurope

© mrtom-uk/iStockphoto.com

Tram on Liberty Bridge

River bus

The BKV transport company runs two routes, every 30 to 60 minutes, 6.30am–8.30pm. Tickets cost Ft750.
- **D 11** (weekdays only): Újpest, Árpád út/Kopaszi-gát.
- **D 12** (weekdays and weekends): Rómaifürdő/Kopaszi-gát.

HÉV trains

The suburban trainline. The following lines operate (the first name indicates the departure station in Buda or Pest):
– **5** Batthyány tér (metro 2)/ Szentendre;
– **6** Közvágóhíd/Ráckeve;
– **7** Boráros tér/Csepel;
– **8** Örs vezér tere (metro 2)/Gödöllő.
– **9** Örs vezér tere (metro 2)/Csömör.

Funicular (Sikló) 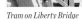 *p. 14.*

Chairlift (Libegő) *p. 76.*

RESTAURANTS

The city has plenty of choice, with different types of restaurants:
– **étterem:** a classic restaurant offering, with fixed-price menus and à la carte;
– **büfé:** fast-food counter service (sandwiches, cakes, hot and cold drinks);
– **vendéglő:** a traditional Hungarian-style restaurant. Once you are seated and presented with a menu, you will be asked for your drinks order.
Tipping p. 121.

A traditional meal usually includes soup, a main course, dessert, a drink and coffee (capuccino or espresso) to finish.

꙰ *Goulash and Paprika p. 135, Where to eat p. 82 & the detachable map on the inside cover for restaurant recommendations. Michelin's 'Main Cities of Europe' guide, also suggests a number of Budapest restaurants, some with Michelin stars.*

SMOKING

Tobacconists (*Nemzeti Dohánybolt*, shops featuring a logo with a green 'T' and '18') are the only places that sell cigarettes. Smoking is prohibited in public spaces (restaurants, theatres, cafés, pubs, on public transport and at their stops, in stations, etc.) but is still permitted on café and restaurant terraces. The same rules apply for vaping as for tobacco.

TAXIS

Taxis (yellow) are plentiful (operating as companies or independently). Ask the price at the start of your journey and keep an eye on the total. Beware of scams, especially if you hail one in the street. The tariff is not higher at night. It's best to book taxis in advance with a reputable company, such as listed below. Their name should appear on the car door or on the luminous sign on the roof.

City Taxi – ℘ (1) 211 1111.
Főtaxi – ℘ (1) 222 2222.
Budapest Taxi – ℘ (1) 777 7777.
6X6 Taxi – ℘ (1) 666 6666.
꙰ *Getting to Budapest p. 3.*

TELEPHONES

From outside Hungary
℘ 00 + 36 (dialling code for Hungary) + 1 (dialling code for Budapest).
From Budapest
To the UK: ℘ 00 + 44 (plus the UK number without the leading 0).
To the Republic of Ireland: ℘ 00 + 353 (plus area code + local number).
To USA/Canada: ℘ 00 + 1 (plus area code and local number).
To Australia: ℘ 00 + 61 (plus area code and local number).

Within Hungary
℘ 06 + town code + local number.

Within Budapest
Simply dial the 7 digits of the phone number without the city code.

Mobile/cell phones
Roaming charges no longer apply within the EU. Calls, SMS messages and internet access are normally included in your tariff and are charged at the same rate as in the country of origin. Some operators still charge for some calls, so check ahead of trip.

TIPPING

A service charge (around 10–15 per cent) is often not included in the bill – look for *szervizdíj* on the menu. A cash tip is therefore usually left at your own discretion.

WIFI

Most bars, cafés, restaurants and hotels offer free access upon request for the code (if it is not shown).

Festivals and events

ANNUAL EVENTS

March
▶**Chamber Music Festival – Gödöllő Palace** (♿ *p. 78*).
www.kiralyikastely.hu

April
▶**Budapest Spring Festival –**
Classical and modern music, theatre, opera, operettas, folk music, Hungarian and foreign ballet, film.
www.btf.hu/events

Sziget Festival

May–June
▶**Jewish Art Festival** – Concerts, poetry readings, theatre in multiple locations across the city.
zsidomuveszetinapok.hu

Mid-June
▶**Danube Carnival** – International dance and music festival (classic, contemporary, traditional Hungarian folk, world). dunakarneval.hu
▶**Night of the Museums** – Free access to museums and entertainment 6pm–1am around 20–25 June.
muzej.hu

July
▶**Open-air film festival** – Daily 4.30pm–11pm, films projected at various outdoor venues.

July–October
▶**Sparties** – Spa parties are held on Saturday evenings at Széchenyi Baths. (♿ *p. 106*), www.bathsbudapest.com
▶**Summer Music Festival – Vajdahunyad Castle** (♿ *p. 55*).
Classical music, klezmer (Jewish folk music), Romani and swing music in the castle courtyard.
www.vajdahunyadcastle.com

August
▶**Sziget Festival** – Mid-August. A Woodstock-style music festival with a dozen stages lasting a week, it attracts young people from around the world to Óbuda Island where

anything goes, in particular good music! www.szigetfestival.com

▶**Festival of Folk Arts** – Held in Buda's Castle District. The city celebrates its birthday with a firework display on 20 August (**♿** *p. 30*). www.mestersegekunnepe.hu

▶**Baroque Festival – Gödöllő Palace** (**♿** *p. 78*). Dance performances, concerts and equestrian displays. www.kiralyikastely.hu

September
▶**Budapest Wine Festival** – Second week. A celebration of wine with auctions, tasting, harvest procession and concerts on the terraces of Buda Castle. ▶

European Heritage Open Days – Third weekend. Access to a number of locations usually closed to the public with conferences and concerts.

October
▶**Café Budapest Contemporary Arts Festival** – Experimental contemporary art (music, film, exhibitions). https://cáfébudapestfest.hu

▶**International Harp Festival** – **Gödöllő Palace** (**♿** *p. 78*) – Beautiful music in a beautiful setting. www.kiralyikastely.hu

December
▶**Christmas markets** – City centre. **Gypsy Philharmonic Orchestra concert** – 30 December, New Year gala with the 100-member Gypsy Orchestra in the Budapest Congress Centre. www.100violins.com

▶**Gala and Ball** – A New Year's Eve concert and party, usually held at the Hungarian State Opera House. www.opera.hu

TEMPORARY EXHIBITIONS

In addition to the museums, a number of galleries and exhibition spaces also hold temporary exhibitions.

Exhibition spaces
Műcsarnok (Hall of Art) – Contemporary art (**♿** *p. 54*).
Mai Manó Ház, Magyar Fotográfusok Háza (Hungarian House of Photography) – Photography exhibitions (**♿** *p. 46*).
Robert Capa Contemporary Photography Center– (formerly the Ernst Museum) Nagymező utca 8 – **Ⓜ** 1 Opera – **🚋** 4, 6 Király utca – trolley bus 70 Akácfa utca – capacenter.hu/en/ – Tue–Sun 11am–7pm, closed Mon. Exhibitions shown in the Night of the Museums programme.

Art galleries
Kogart House – Andrássy út 112 – **Ⓜ** 1 Bajza utca – www.kogart.hu – Daily 10am–5pm (closed weekends).
Várfok Galéria – Várfok utca 11 & 14 – **Ⓜ** 2 Széll Kálmán tér – www.varfok-galeria.hu – Tue–Fri 11am–6pm (closed Sun & Mon).
Godot Galéria – Bartók Béla út 11 – **Ⓜ** 4 Szent Gellért tér – www.godot.hu – Tue–Fri 9am–2pm, Sat 10am–1pm.

Find out more

125

Goulash
© Hungarian Tourism Agency

Key dates

1–4C AD – The **Romans** found the province of Pannonia (in the west of present-day Hungary).
Aquincum becomes a flourishing city.
5C AD – The **Huns** capture Aquincum.
896 – The **Magyars** cross the Carpathian mountains.
Prince Árpád sets up his summer camp on Csepel Island.
1241 – Buda and Pest are devastated by the **Tartar** invasion.
1243 – **King Béla IV** builds Buda Castle (⟲ *p. 14*).
1458–1490 – Under the reign of **Matthias Corvinus** (Matthias I), Buda becomes one of Europe's cultural centres.
1541 – The **Turks** conquer Buda.
1686 – The Christian armies led by Habsburg Prince **Charles of Lorraine** liberate the city. Buda becomes a garrison for the Austrian army.
1825 – Count **István Széchenyi** builds the Chain Bridge.
1848–1849 – **Hungarian Revolution** against the Habsburgs.
1867 – Austro-Hungarian compromise and creation of the Dual Monarchy: **Emperor Franz Joseph of Austria** and his wife **Elisabeth** are crowned sovereigns of Hungary.
1873 – The unification of Buda, Pest and Óbuda as one city: Budapest.
1896 – Opening of the first metro line (present-day M 1) in continental Europe. Millennial celebrations for the Magyar conquest.
1904 – Grand opening of Parliament.

126

1920 – Treaty of Trianon redefines the Hungarian borders, after separation from Austria in 1918.
1944 – Reign of terror by the Arrow Cross Party (⟲ *p. 62*), allies of the German Nazis.
1945 – The Russian Red Army liberates the city from the Germans at the end of the Second World War.
1949 – Communist minister **László Rajk** is tried and executed by the Soviet-influenced regime.
23 October–November 1956 – Popular uprising. **Imre Nagy** (prime minister 1953–55) returns to power in November and announces, among other measures, neutrality and withdrawal from the Warsaw Pact. Soviet tanks enter the city and crush the uprising, an estimated 3,000 are killed. The city is devastated; 200,000 Hungarians leave the country.
1989 – Rehabilitation of Imre Nagy (executed in 1958). He is reburied with full honours.
23 October 1989 – the People's Republic of Hungary becomes the **Republic of Hungary**. Red stars disappear from public buildings.
1991 – Last of the Russian troops leave Budapest.
2004 – Hungary joins the European Union .
From 2010 – The Hungarian political landscape changes: Fidesz, the right-wing party led by **Viktor Orbán**, returning prime minister in 2010 and re-elected in 2018. He enacts a new constitution in 2012.

Urban planning

ÓBUDA, BUDA AND PEST

In the 1st century AD, the early Celtic settlement was occupied by the Romans, who established a military camp in Óbuda and a civilian town in **Aquincum** (👣 *p. 75*), on the right bank of the Danube. Invasions followed and the Huns ousted the Romans in the 5C. Legend has it that the town owes its name to Attila the Hun's brother, who sometimes went by the name of Buda. The town continued to develop on the right bank with the construction in the 13C of the first fortress on the rocky spur of Buda. Under Ottoman rule, in the 16C, most of the population was concentrated in Pest, on the left bank. Most of Buda's churches became mosques and Turkish baths began to proliferate. In the 19C, Count **István Széchenyi** (1791–1860) developed a number of urbanisation projects, including the Chain Bridge, the National Theatre (in Pest) and introduced steam shipping on the River Danube. Archduke Joseph, the popular palatine of Hungary, directed the Pest Beautification Commission (1808), but the project for Buda was less successful.

GOLDEN AGE

At the turn of the 20C, under the Austro-Hungarian Empire, Budapest became a flourishing industrial metropolis. Óbuda, Buda and Pest were officially united in 1873. The population grew with the arrival of a large number of Jews from Eastern Europe, most of whom settled in the Erzsébetváros district of Pest. With the economy expanding and projects abounding, an international urban planning competition was held in order to regulate development in the capital. Two key projects were approved: the **Andrássy út** radial avenue (👣 *p. 44*) and Nagykörút (Grand Boulevard). Work began in 1894. A huge national millennial exhibition was organised in Városliget (City Park) in 1896 to mark the conquest 1,000 years earlier of the Carpathian Basin by the Magyar tribes. In the same year the first metro in Europe opened, but the pinnacle of achievement for the age came in 1902 with the construction of the **Parliament Building**, inspired by the Houses of Parliament in London (👣 *p. 38*).

THE DARK YEARS

With the collapse of the Austro-Hungarian Empire after the First World War, Budapest's golden age came to an end. During its time under the authoritarian regime of Admiral Miklós Horthy, the city regained some of its pre-war momentum, but this respite was cut short a few years later by the Nazi reign of terror in the ghetto of Budapest. The Second World War saw the destruction of all the city's bridges, Buda Castle and the Old Town, which was not rebuilt until the 1960s. During the communist era, a hasty and enforced industrialisation led to a fifth of the country's population being crammed into the city, leading to a lack of housing and an increase in pollution that had serious consequences, with a fallout for the capital that is still being felt today. Any construction programmes that were undertaken seemed to be conducted without any real or at least visible organisation.

A CITY AWAKES

Following the fall of the Berlin Wall and the arrival of democracy in Hungary, the city was on the move again. On a symbolic level, Communist signs were removed from official buildings and one by one the streets gradually reverted to their original names. Traffic was relieved by a bypass and major building works were undertaken, particularly in the tourism, commerce and service industries. However, Budapest still does not have an urban policy befitting a capital city. For example, construction of the National Theatre, which was part of a national design contest, was planned for Erzsébet tér, but was interrupted by the 1998 elections. The theatre was finally built near the Rákoczi Bridge, on the Pest side, and opened in 2002. It formed part of a new district built on the site planned for the World Expo 96.

PRIVATE INITIATIVES

A significant building programme of restoration work in both Buda and Pest was embarked upon in the 1990s, notably in the **Belváros** area (between Szabad S. út and József A. utca). The facelift given to Deák Ferenc utca (so-called Fashion Street), was thanks to investment by the Hungarian businessman, Péter Csipak. Several reconstruction projects in **Erzsébetváros** were the result of foreign investment. Among contemporary Hungarian architects, the name of **József Finta** crops up frequently. While working under the Communist regime, Finta had already acquired a reputation for designing some of the large hotels on the banks of the Danube. Working with Antal Puhl Associates, Finta then designed the Kempinski Hotel Corvinus on Erzsébet tér, a unique building in a C-shape that blazed its own contemporary trail and opened in 1992. He also designed the circular Police Headquarters building on Teve utca in 1997. Also opened in 1992, the French Institute on the banks of the Danube was designed by France's Georges Maurios. Its cladding protects it from pollution and it fits well into the urban environment. The current century was ushered in with the construction of the head offices of the Dutch **ING Bank** in 2004, with a striking hyperkinetic façade (♿ *p. 49*) and the CET shopping and cultural centre designed by Dutch architect Kas Oosterhuis and renamed 'the Whale' (**Bálna**, ♿ *p. 68*) due to its rounded shape.

Secession Movement and Art Nouveau

THE PUSH TOWARDS MODERNITY

The second half of the 19C was marked by several key events which formed part of a remarkable push towards modernity in Budapest. In 1867, after two centuries of Austrian domination, Hungary was finally recognised as an independent nation. The unified city of Budapest was 'born' in 1873 and in 1896 the country's thousandth anniversary was celebrated. The city prospered, industry boomed, the population grew, the standard of living increased and education improved, giving rise to new schools, theatres and an opera house. All eyes were upon Budapest: major civil engineering works were commissioned, notably the first underground railway in continental Europe. And the city acquired one of the largest stock exchanges in Europe and one of the largest parliament buildings in the world. And with this revival came a profound national spirit, which translated into the glorifying of heroic national events and found expression in Romantic scholasticism and idealised classicism. The painting *Hungarian Conquest* by artist Mihály Munkácsy, commissioned for the Budapest Parliament Building, exemplified this style of official art.

NATIONAL ART

At the turn of the 20C century, this academic 'historicism' was largely rejected by Hungarian art circles, and 1896 saw the advent of Secessionist architecture, with the millennial celebrations providing impetus for the development of a national artistic style based on the Magyar origins of the Hungarian population. Social, ethical and utopian ideas came to be expressed through art, at the same time paving the way for a future society. New artistic trends, influenced by the evolution of European art, made their way across Hungary: naturalism and painting *en plein air*, Art Nouveau and symbolism. Hungary was in full artistic swing, the roots of which lay in a number of individual experiences. Styles were sometimes wholly in opposition but found unity in their mutual rejection of the formalism of academic art.

ART NOUVEAU, AN EXPRESSION OF MODERNITY

The Art Nouveau movement exploded and embodied a new modern spirit. A major international art trend, in Hungary it acquired a distinctive character all of its own. The Hungarian Art Nouveau movement, also known as Secessionism

(Szecesszió), took its inspiration from the rediscovered medieval and folk architecture of Transylvania and Scandinavia. The pioneer was without doubt the famous Hungarian architect **Ödön Lechner** (1845–1914). In the 1890s, he established a new form of architecture, harking back to the origins of the Hungarian people from the east. He was inspired by eastern motifs and architectural forms along with rural folk art, in particular Hungarian tapestries. He used tiles produced in the famous Zsolnay factory in Pécs to decorate the roofs and façades of his buildings, clothing them in a kind of ornate national costume. He emphasized his own artistic style with the **Museum of Applied Arts** (🕯 *p. 66*), built between 1891 and 1896 and at the margins of the classic conceptions of the era. The east, evoking the Asiatic origins of the Magyar people, was very evident in his first modern steel constructions: the foyer of the museum is decorated with tiles showing eastern motifs and the spectacular atrium features Islamic double aracades, a wonderful cupola and terracotta tiles, also evoking the Orient (it is set to reopen in 2020 with a new modern wing).

THE VIENNESE INFLUENCE

The Viennese Secession movement had a strong influence on a number of buildings in Budapest, including **Gresham Palace** (🕯*p. 43*) and the **Géllert Spa Hotel** (🕯*p. 31*). Its influence is also evident in the works of Ödön Lechner; the organic shapes and graceful, flowing lines in the entrance hall of the **Museum of Applied Arts** are typical of the Art Nouveau movement, as is the former **Postal Savings Bank building** (🕯 *p. 40*), built between 1899 and 1902. The flamboyant façade is decorated with mosaics featuring beehive and flower motifs and displays great technical and artistic skill. The ceramic tiles on the roof are decorated with floral and animal motifs, while mythological references abound, reflecting the fashionable national spirit of the time, as do the two bulls' heads that reference the Hungarian legend of 'Attila's Treasure'.

TO EACH HIS OR HER OWN

From 1905 onwards, architecture assumed a social character. Still leaning on Ödön Lechner's research, the new generation of architects took on technical and hygiene issues. Their goal was to create a better environment in perfect harmony with nature, as expressed in Hungarian folk art. **Béla Lajta** (1873–1920) combined Hungarian Art Nouveau and brick architecture typical of Scandinavia in his Jewish Institute for the Blind (1905–1908). He mixed traditional Hungarian motifs with resolutely modern architectural elements such as the façade of the **Rózsavölgyi House** (🕯 *p. 60*).

Polymath **Károly Kós** (1883–1977, writer, architect, illustrator, politician) was responsible for re-establishing continuity with the past through his references to the Magyar people and the Huns. In 1908–1909, together with Dezső Zreumeczky, Kós designed

130

Turquoise domes of Budapest Zoo Elephant House, Széchenyi Baths in the background

© devteev/iStockphoto.com

many of the animal houses for **Budapest Zoo** (🕭 *p.54*), conceiving structures in a medieval style that reflected the architectural forms typical of Transylvania (turrets, spires and balconies), reshaped by their collective imagination.

ART INFLUENCES

The concept of communing with the elements was fundamental for the artists of the time. The work of Hungarian painter **Károly Ferenczy** (1862–1917) developed a lyrical approach to nature and man's evolution in harmony with it. He gave art a spiritual sense through which he became closer to European symbolism. In *The Three Magi*, completed in 1898 and exhibited in the National Gallery (🕭 *p. 17)*, man is at one with nature and the aura is mystical, full of the potential for miracles. Ferenczy, known in Hungary as the 'father of Impressionism' was a founding member of the influential Hungarian Nagybánya artists' colony, as was **Simon Hollósy** (1857–1918). Less productive, but interested in naturalism, Hollósy found his own expression in his paintings e*n plein air*, following in the footsteps of French Impressionists and taking inspiration from Transylvanian landscapes, such as in *Landscape in Técső* and *Sunset with Stacks*. His penetrating *Self-portrait* hangs in the National Gallery.

Thermal baths and spas

SOCIAL AND MEDICINAL

You may be surprised to see people walking around Budapest, both day and night, carrying small waterproof bags. Equipped with towel, shampoo and soap they are on their way to, or indeed returning from, the baths *(open from 6am)*. Budapest's many thermal baths are a reminder of the Roman era and the Ottoman occupation and have long been part of daily life for its citizens, who visit them on a regular basis to soothe aches and pains, chat, play chess and simply relax, or, more recently, also to party *(⌀ p. 100)*.

WELLBEING

Thermal waters are well known for their therapeutic properties and their ability to induce a real sense of general wellbeing. The websites of the various baths in Budapest list the facilities on offer at each one and provide details of the pools and temperatures, with many providing massages and extra spa treatments in addition to the Invigorating plunge pools, saunas and steam baths. Don't leave Budapest without visiting the baths, even it if is only to admire the wonderful buildings in which they are housed and marvel at the sheer range of facilities on offer.

MILLENNIAL RITUAL

Budapest and the surrounding area are literally awash with hot springs. They are thought to total more than a hundred, some of which supply the thermal spa complexes in the capital. The healing powers of the waters did not escape the attention of the Romans, who had already acquired the bathing habit and saw no reason not to continue with it in Budapest, bathing regularly, as can be seen from the archeological ruins at Aquincum *(⌀ p. 75)*. The Ottoman invasion of Hungary in the 16C also had a significant effect on the bathing culture in Budapest. During the Turkish occupation, which lasted over a century, the baths were developed further and often on a grand scale, typically with octagonal pools covered with domed roofs. The most well-known and representative in terms of architecure are listed here:

Gellért *(⌀ p. 105)*,
Rudas *(⌀ p. 106)*,
Király *(⌀ p. 106)*,
Lukács *(⌀ p. 106)*,
Széchenyi *(⌀ p. 106)*.

Musical traditions

FOLK

After 1750 Hungarian music was dominated by a new heroic style called *verbunkos*, also known as *hongroise*, traditional dance music usually played by Romani musicians and originally used to encourage young men to sign up to be soldiers. The *verbunkos* tradition lives on in the *csárdás* folk dance, still performed today. At the end of the 18C, musicians in Budapest belonged to a guild and performed religious works, stage music and contemporary operas. They also played Hungarian music and Romani groups would accompany folk dances on the violin.

THE GREAT COMPOSORS

The most famous Hungarian composer is without doubt **Ferenc (Franz) Liszt** (1811–1886), who was inspired by Hungarian folk melodies. Among his works are symphonic poems such as *Les Préludes* (1854), the famous *Hungarian Rhapsodies* (1846–1885) and *Historical Portraits* (1884–1886), works in which Liszt pays tribute to his country. **Ferenc Erkel** (1810–1893) composed the opera *László Hunyadi* in 1844 but reached the height of his compositional powers in 1860 with *Bánk Bán*, often now thought of as Hungary's national opera – and indeed he also composed the music for the national anthem.

Béla Bartók (1881–1945) and **Zoltán Kodály** (1882–1967) returned to the origins of folk music to develop their own style. Bartók achieved worldwide fame whereas Kodály was largely only known in Hungary. His wonderful *Psalmus Hungaricus* (1923) celebrated the fiftieth anniversary of the reunion of Buda with Pest.

The Hungarian operetta gained international acclaim with **Imre Kálmán** (1882–1953), who had his first success in 1908 with *The Mongol Invasion*, but it was **Franz Lehár's** *The Merry Widow* (1870–1948) that immortalized the genre.

AND TODAY...

A number of Budapest's concert halls stage performances of classical music. Famous virtuoso pianists **Zoltán Kocsis** (1952–2016) and **Dezső Ránki** (b. 1951) and composers such as **György Ligeti** (1923–2006) fly the flag for Hungarian musical genius today. Folk music remains popular, both in the capital and internationally, thanks in large part to the Hungarian group **Muzsikás** and their vocalist Márta Sebestyén. In recent years Budapest has also earned its place on the European music scene, particularly with **electronic** and **techno** beats, reaffirming the country's creativity in the world of music.

Literary and grand cafés

MY CAFÉ IS MY CASTLE!

The coffee culture, which has long been entrenched in Budapest life, began with the Turks in the 16C, and by the dawn of the 20C around six hundred cafés were scattered about the streets of Budapest. As in Vienna and Paris, the belle époque saw the literary café reach the height of popularity. In 1914 the Hungarian poet and prose-writer Dezső Kosztolányi wrote that an Englishman may declare with unbridled pride that his house is his castle, but a citizen of Budapest will counter that his castle is his café. And it was true that for the many people struggling with the limitations of housing in Budapest, the café often became a second home.

A LITERARY ATMOSPHERE

The haunt of writers and journalists in the 19C, cafés played a key role in the flourishing of Hungarian literature, sometimes even morphing into editing and newsrooms. And many of these old establishments frequented by turn-of-the century café society are still open today, in particular those on Andrássy and Rákóczi út. People come to chat and read the papers and reviews supplied for regulars in different languages, and sometimes to play a little billiards.

SURVIVORS

The end of the First World War saw the number of cafés decline dramatically, leaving a deep void at the heart of the city's population. After the Second World War, many cafés such as Belvárosi opened their doors once more but it was never quite the same.

As Jenő Heltai expressed so eloquently in 1949 in *Szemtanú*: 'When I look at the terrible tragedy of cafés, at the way in which they flourished and then declined, I feel rather like the legendary character Rip Van Winkle, who awoke from a twenty-year sleep and examined the world around him. The old man searched in vain for the cafés of his youth, where he had felt so at home. Cafés went from stars of the show to bit players.'

Despite this, some cafés still linger, their decor and furnishings providing an idea of how they were in their heyday: **Café Gerbeaud** (🛈 *p. 61*) and **New York Café** (🛈 *p. 64*).

Goulash and paprika

Hungarian cuisine, full of flavour and spice yet gentle on the palate, has resumed the long journey originally taken by the Asian Magyars. Thanks to the nomadic heritage of the Turks, Bavarians and Bulgarians a culinary cross-fertilisation has taken place. The Austro-Hungarian influence is most evident in the art of patisserie, although as elsewhere in the world, the people of Budapest are not immune to the delights of kebabs, pizzas and burgers.

TYPICAL DISHES

Ingredients: The local cuisine makes frequent use of a roux, to which a very generous amount of onions are added, forming the basis of a sauce that is then highly spiced with the *piros arany* or 'red gold' of **paprika**. This spice is both ubiquitous and dominant, to the point that all dishes made with it are called *paprikás*, in particular those made with fish, poultry and veal.

Starters: *Pogácsa*, introduced by the Turks, are small crispy, salted scones made with wheat flour or potato and containing lard along with cheese or spices.

Main dishes: Soup is a standard dish in Hungarian cuisine, in particular *Jókai bableves*, which is named after the famous 19C Hungarian novelist and revolutionary Mór Jókai; it is a rich bean soup with strips of smoked pork and sausage. *Hortobágyi húsos palacsinta* is a thick savoury **pancake**, filled with meat and onions.

Soup and meat: The most famous Hungarian dish is *gulyás*, a **beef soup** with onions and paprika, and sometimes also potatoes or carrots. Goulash as it is generally understood outside Hungary is called *pörkölt* within it: a **stew** made with braised, boneless meat, tomatoes and green peppers, with a pronounced taste of onion. *Tokány* is another version of stew in which the paprika is replaced with pepper. Roasted pork shank (*csülök*) is also very popular and features prominently on the menus of many small restaurants. The Hungarian Great Plain is the source of a number of different poultry dishes, such as chicken with paprika (*csirkepaprikás*) and chicken soup (*újházi tyúkhúsleves*), made with peas, mushrooms, carrots and pasta.

Foie gras is served either sliced or fried in large cubes, in the fat of the goose itself, with a little garlic and onion. There is a huge array of excellent **sausages**, in particular top-notch salami.

Vegetables: Dishes are often served with rice, homemade pasta often fashioned into dumplings (*galuska*) or a mix of flour and eggs rolled into small balls that are roasted (*tarhonya*). Green vegetables are not generally served, except in top restaurants. If salad is on the menu, it will normally feature cucumbers, pickled cabbage or peppers in vinegar.

Fish: The most common is **pike-perch** or *fogas*. Other fish on the menu include sturgeon (*tok*) from the Tisza river and carp (*ponty*), served in breadcrumbs in traditional Serbian style, with a sprinkling of paprika. *Halászlé* is a **soup** made only with freshwater fish, including carp, catfish and pike. This tasty stew includes onion and Hungarians often add a diced pepper. In some restaurants, particularly during the summer, it is made outside in huge cauldrons and can be very highly spiced.

DESSERTS AND SWEETS

Crêpes: *Palacsinta* are similar to French crêpes; they are served with a wide variety of fillings such as sweetened cottage cheese, ground walnuts or apricot jam.

Cakes: Pastries made with poppy seeds, apple or nuts are traditional in Central Europe. *Túrós* is a kind of cheesecake, but looks rather uninteresting next to a piece of *dobos torta*. Invented by the famous pastry chef József Dobos, this is a layered sponge cake with rich chocolate buttercream, cut into slices, each one topped with an orange caramel glaze and sides covered in ground hazelnuts.

Rigó jancsi is a chocolate sponge cake made of two thin layers with a rich chocolate filling in the middle. You may find it hard to resist *somlói galuska* made with several layers of sponge (plain, cocoa and ground walnuts) with raisins and a rum syrup, served with whipped cream. *Rétes* is a strudel stuffed with

apples, quark, poppyseeds, nuts and cherries. The very popula *túró rudi* is a chocolate bar filled with curd and comes in different flavours and sizes. *Kürtöskalács* ('chimney cake') is a spit cake baked on an open fire, cylindrical in shape and made with pastry dough, served plain or with a sprinkling of sugar, cinnamon or chocolate.

WINES AND ALCOHOL

Wine: Hungary's vineyards date back to Roman times and the country boasts the largest wine-growing area in Central Europe. **Tokaji** (Tokay), a sweet liqueur wine that is golden in colour, is the country's best known wine. **Tokaji aszú** is a delicious sweet wine and and holds its own among the world's most famous wines. Produced since the 16C, it was the first dessert wine to be made with dried grapes. The red wines of the **Villány** region are equally renowned.

Spirits: Hungarians rarely drink wine at lunchtime but schnapps is extremely popular. *Barack pálinka*, an apricot schnapps from Kecskemét, is a national drink. *Puszta* is a delicious cocktail made with Tokaji, **apricot schnapps** and a herbal liqueur.

Unicum is a branded herbal liqueur or bitters, made to a secret formula using forty herbal plants. It dates back to 1790 when the medicinal bitters were used to treat Emperor Joseph II of Austria.

Beer: on tap or bottled, beer (*sör*) is very popular and widely available with local brands including Dréher, Soproni and Borsodi.

Index

137

139

142

Photo credits

Page 4

Parliament: © René Mattes/hemis.fr
Chain Bridge: © alle12/iStockphoto.com
Museum of Fine Arts: © _ultraforma_/iStockphoto.com
Gellért Baths: © Hungarian Tourism Agency
Castle district: © Photoservice/iStockphoto.com

Page 5

Buda Castle: © Vladislav Zolotov/iStockphoto.com
Dohány Street Synagogue: © Arpad Benedek/iStockphoto.com
Széchenyi Baths: © BFTK Budapesti Fesztivál- és Turisztikai Központ
State Opera House: © Hungarian Tourism Agency
Café New York: © Hungarian Tourism Agency

Maps

Inside

Buda Castle   *p16*
Várnegyed   *p21*

Cover

Districts of Budapest
   inside front cover

Detachable map

Budapest   *front*
Public Transport   *back*

THE GREEN GUIDE short-stays **Budapest**

Editorial Director	Cynthia Ochterbeck
Editor	Sophie Friedman
Editorial	Jackie Strachan, Jane Moseley
Production Manager	Natasha George
Cartography	Peter Wrenn, Theodor Cepraga
Picture Editor	Yoshimi Kanazawa
Interior Design	Laurent Muller
Layout	Natasha George

Contact Us	Michelin Travel and Lifestyle North America
	One Parkway South
	Greenville, SC 29615
	USA
	travel.lifestyle@us.michelin.com
	Michelin Travel Partner
	Hannay House
	39 Clarendon Road
	Watford, Herts WD17 1JA
	UK
	☏01923 205240
	travelpubsales@uk.michelin.com
	www.viamichelin.co.uk

Special Sales	For information regarding bulk sales,
	customized editions and premium sales,
	please contact us at:
	travel.lifestyle@us.michelin.com

Note to the reader Addresses, phone numbers, opening hours and prices published in this guide are accurate at the time of press. We welcome corrections and suggestions that may assist us in preparing the next edition. While every effort is made to ensure that all information printed in this guide is correct and up-to-date, Michelin Travel Partner accepts no liability for any direct, indirect or consequential losses howsoever caused so far as such can be excluded by law.

**YOUR OPINION IS ESSENTIAL
TO IMPROVING OUR PRODUCTS**

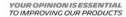

*Help us by answering the
questionnaire on our website:*
satisfaction.michelin.com

Michelin Travel Partner

Société par actions simplifiées au capital de 15 044 940 EUR
27 cours de l'Ile Seguin - 92100 Boulogne Billancourt (France)
R.C.S. Nanterre 433 677 721

No part of this publication may be reproduced in any form
without the prior permission of the publisher.

© Michelin Travel Partner
ISBN 978-2-067241-17-6
Printed: April 2019
Printer: Estimprim

Although the information in this guide was believed by the authors and publisher to be accurate
and current at the time of publication, they cannot accept responsibility for any inconvenience,
loss, or injury sustained by any person relying on information or advice contained in this guide.
Things change over time and travellers should take steps to verify and confirm information,
especially time-sensitive information related to prices, hours of operation and availability.